THE POCKET GUIDE TO

PRODUCT
LAUNCHES

THE POCKET GUIDE TO

PRODUCT LAUNCHES

GET CONFIDENT,

GO TO MARKET, AND WIN

MARY SHEEHAN

The Pocket Guide to Product Launches

Get Confident, Go to Market, and Win

ISBN 978-1-5445-2760-4 Paperback
      978-1-5445-2761-1 Ebook

To access additional
The Pocket Guide to Product Marketing resources,
please visit Productlaunch.pro.

CONTENTS

PART 6

INTRODUCTION

The launch is a definitive moment in the life of a product and can often make or break its success. But don't worry, it's not rocket science. What a successful launch really comes down to is strict organization, effective communication, and a dash of creativity. This book will prepare you for a successful launch.

Product marketing is one of the most rewarding, and challenging, roles in tech. I've also found it's one of the hardest roles to become proficient in. I have seen countless new product marketers struggle in the early months of the role. Compounding this, there aren't any college courses on product marketing, and often, the role is of the "learn on the job" type. This book is for new product marketers (or those newly running product launches) to quickly get up to speed on product launches, one of the core functions of the role. It's something I desperately wish existed back when I was starting out.

This book pulls together templates, lists, and tips that I've gleaned over 10 years launching products. I've led over 250 product and feature launches and have seen what makes the difference between a successful launch and one that flops. Throughout this book, I outline the top steps you'll need to take to have a successful launch, from creating a solid plan, to gathering the right team, to communicating and measuring the results. I've included real examples from my own career to highlight what has worked and what doesn't from companies like Google, Adobe, and the startup world. The skillset you will develop by running launches adds tools to your growing toolkit, which will eventually make you an expert in the product marketing field. To help you pinpoint the biggest insights, you'll find "Launch Learnings" throughout the book to help you remember the key points.

Each section of this book is formatted to help you become knowledgeable quickly, and the supporting documents on the website Productlaunch.pro will help you execute the launch plans with ease. My hope is that you will continue to use the book and resources as a reference guide even after your first launch.

HOW TO USE THIS BOOK

This book is organized by chapters on the most important aspects of running a product launch. Read it all at once, or choose the chapters that you need more help with and start there. Here's a quick overview.

Part 1: Develop the Go-to-Market Plan

In this critical section of the book, you'll get the skills to develop your first soup to nuts go-to-market (GTM) plan, including an introduction to your new best friend, the GTM template.

Part 2: Know Your Target Market (Your Customer)

It may sound obvious, but understanding your target market is a crucial part of the launch process. Many products and campaigns are launched without first considering who the ideal target is. This section will walk you through the importance of understanding who your product is for and how to uncover insights about them to make your launch more effective.

Part 3: Align the Team and Internal Communication

Every launch is only as good as the team behind it. Whether you're a team of 1 or 100, this section explores how to identify each person's ownership and make sure communication is as effective as possible.

Part 4: Prime the Positioning and Messaging

This chapter explores the difference between positioning and messaging and how to get started with communicating the value of your launch.

Part 5: Define the Metrics That Matter

If you don't have the right goals for your launch, who cares? Get your stakeholders to collaborate on the right goals and metrics that level up to your existing business goals.

Part 6: Nail the Launch Timing

Hands down, the most difficult thing to master with a GTM plan is the timing of the launch, or the "go live" date. In the digital world, so much is up in the air, and timing can be really fluid. This chapter helps you get the launch timing as tight as possible and gives hints to help you when something goes wrong. I also share how to keep up the post-launch momentum.

Resources and Appendix

Here, I share some continued resources to get you up to speed quickly and in touch with other product marketing communities.

* * *

I hope this book helps you get organized and feel more confident so you can run a great launch that you're proud of and can repeat over and over again. Make sure you visit Productlaunch.pro to get the free GTM plan; it's a great way to follow along.

Since this is for YOU, please let me know how it can be better. I'd love to hear from you and look forward to any feedback, questions, or comments, especially regarding your experience using this book and the templates. I'd also love to hear more examples for future versions of the book. This has been a great passion project for me, and I hope you enjoy it. Please feel free to reach me directly for comments, questions, and reprint permissions at MaryShirleySheehan@gmail.com.

Thank you so much for your support in buying this book. I really appreciate it!

—Mary Sheehan

PART 1

DEVELOP THE GO-TO-MARKET PLAN

"You have to ruthlessly prioritize."
—**Katrina Lake**, CEO, StitchFix

According to the late Clayton Christensen, the legendary Harvard Business School professor and author, over 30,000 new products are brought to market each year, and 95 percent fail. Why? The reasons are limitless. You could have the wrong product for the market, not enough financing, or the inability to promote the product to the right people. However, I would argue that much of a product's success comes down to *how* that product is launched, and as product marketers, this is something we have a lot of control over. It all starts with the go-to-market, or GTM, plan.

> *"Over 30,000 new products brought to market each year, and 95 percent fail."*
>
> —Clayton Christensen

A GTM plan is a blueprint that details the strategy of how a company will target its existing customers and prospective customers with its value prop and differentiation from the competition with a product. It's essentially the launch playbook complete with milestones, a checklist, and goal tracking that is shared with all stakeholders and updated at least weekly. It's more than just a glorified checklist; it's your strategy of how you'll win against the competition with this launch, how you'll track goals and milestones, and how you'll effectively communicate your product launch. In addition, it's your "single source of truth" for the next several months until launch. A product marketing manager should own creating and updating this document, but when there is not one at a company, anyone from the product manager to the founder can manage this.

LAUNCH LEARNING: The go-to-market (GTM) plan is more than a checklist; it's the strategy for how a company will target its existing customers and prospective customers with its value prop and differentiation from the competition with a product.

I have used iterations of the following GTM plan to launch hundreds of new products. If you do not have a process for launching products, launches tend to come together at the last minute and not very well. If there are not any milestones or gates, products will launch to the world when the engineers and product managers are able to release them, which as you can imagine, leaves marketing and sales scrambling and customers confused. Putting this plan in place brings accountability to the organization and ensures you will meet your deadlines. It also gives the leadership team the confidence that you know what you are doing and have a plan.

LAUNCH LEARNING: Without a GTM plan, new products in market will leave marketing and sales scrambling and customers confused.

DEVELOP YOUR LAUNCH STRATEGY

Before you sit down and put pen to paper, it's critical to develop a strong strategy for your launch, or at least one that others can debate. What is a launch strategy? It's a plan of action for your product launch, which includes the who, what, where, when, and why of the launch. A great strategy also considers what you are NOT focusing on. I'll talk about this in detail in Part 2, but as an example, specifying the audience for the launch (and who it is NOT for) is an important part of your launch strategy. The strategy helps to define all of the biggest pieces of the launch in a digestible way that you can share with stakeholders. This will be your North Star and should be set and approved by your team members and any executives who have an interest in the launch. This gives more context on the launch strategy and can be filled in on the first tab of your GTM plan:

- **(Who) Target market**—The launch audience, defined as specifically as possible with research. Discussed in detail in Part 2.
- **(Who—internal) The internal launch team**— Tips for getting the right team and managing them well using the Responsible, Accountable, Consulted, Informed (RACI) principles. See Part 4.
- **(What) Product stage**—Is your product in alpha, beta, or beyond? See details later in Part 1.
- **(When) Launch milestones**—Stepping-stones to get to your launch date, as outlined in Part 6.
- **(Where) Top launch channels**—The top external and internal channels you will be communicating this launch to, so anyone reading your document can grasp this quickly.
- **(Why) Goals**—What are the top metrics that will drive your launch plan? See Part 6 for more details.

Example of the key info tab of the GTM plan:

Team	Responsible	Accountable	Consulted	Informed
PMM	PMM	—	—	—
Project Management	PM	—	—	—
Sales	Project Specialist	—	—	—
Other Teams	Legal	—	—	—
Roll-Out Timing and Goals				
Timing	FY21QX or MM/DD	FY21QX or MM/DD	FY21QX or MM/DD	FY21QX or MM/DD
Product Stage	Alpha	Alpha	Alpha	Alpha
Target Audience	XYZ	XYZ	XYZ	XYZ
Milestones	123	123	123	123
Goals	—	—	—	—
Launch Date				

GTM Strategy Example from Google

I ran my first massive launch at Google to bring to market a highly anticipated advertising product known as Viewable Impressions for our advertisers and publishers. The product answered previously unknown questions for digital marketers: *Did anyone see my advertisement online? How much of my ad did they see?* Although the launch was complicated and had many different stakeholders across many different teams, on the marketing end, it went without a hitch because our strategy was clear and we set it from the beginning. We got tons of press, including a front-page article on *The New York Times* with our then-VP of Product, Neal Mohan (now Chief Product Officer of YouTube). Here's a peek into what our strategy looked like:

- **(Who) Target market**—Existing Google advertisers and publishers spending over the minimum threshold.
- **(Who—internal) The internal launch team**—This was a heavily detailed list including product marketers, product managers, and sales specialists. We also had an executive sponsor to make sure we stayed on track.
- **(What) Product stage**—We launched originally in beta (as many Google products do) to give us

flexibility to make updates as we rolled out the full product.

- **(When) Launch milestones**—We launched to advertisers in the United States first, then advertisers in select regions, then globally. We followed suit with the same strategy for our publisher audience, which included a complementary product.

- **(Where) Top launch channels**—

  » **Owned channels**—At Google, we were lucky to have a well-followed blog as well as newsletter, and I made sure to plug our launch announcement into these channels the day of the launch.

  » **Internal enablement**—We had a large internal enablement plan as well with trainings, case studies, and sales decks ready to go on the launch date.

  » **Press**—Because this was such a big game-changer for our industry, we had a thorough press plan (which landed us on the front page of the *Financial Times*). This also included a partnership with a governing body called the IAB (Interactive Advertising Bureau) that helped to lend us some credibility. Press isn't always available, especially at small companies, so I'll discuss some other ways to make an impact throughout this book.

- » **Events**—We had a major events strategy, speaking at many of the largest industry events over the 3–6 months post launch and at some smaller customer events as well.
- **(Why) Goals**—Our goal was to drive adoption for this product over the course of a 12-month period, which also helped us exceed our quarterly targets and annual recurring revenue (ARR) goals.

Because we had this thorough plan, we were able to easily develop our launch checklist, regularly update internal stakeholders, and make sure the launch was successful when it went to market. Don't despair if you don't have the resources of Google. This is just one example, and I'll share many other "scrappier" examples throughout this book.

SHOULD YOU LAUNCH?

Let me ask you a seemingly simple question—*Should* you launch? If you've purchased this book, you've probably already discerned that you need to do a product launch or at least some communication about a product. But it's always a great idea to take a step back and ask yourself, Why are we launching? And why now?

Sometimes you may get pressure from the engineering or product teams to enable a product launch for something they've built that may not warrant a product launch. For example, it may not be "launch worthy" if they have worked on a back-end software improvement, increased the speed of the product, or otherwise impacted the product in a way that a customer won't necessarily "see." These improvements are essential and should be celebrated at the internal company all-hands, but they may not warrant a marketing launch.

If you can answer two or more of these questions positively, you likely need a product launch:

- ✓ Do you have product adoption, usage, and/or revenue goals?
- ✓ Have customers been asking for this product or feature?
- ✓ Is this a game changer for your industry?
- ✓ Can a customer or prospect purchase what you are releasing (vs. a free feature update)?
- ✓ Will the external release of this product or feature help your competitive position in the market?

If you're still convinced you need a product launch after reviewing this list, it might be time to put the plan into action.

Set Goals Now

It's important to set the goals for your launch at the *start* of launch planning. Often, these goals are driven by more than just the person managing the launch and should align the launch activities to real business objectives. According to the *State of Product Marketing 2020* report produced by the Product Marketing Alliance, bottom-line KPIs are a top priority for product marketers. Specifically, 56 percent of product marketers are measured by generating revenue, 44 percent are responsible for increasing marketing qualified leads (MQLs), and 36 percent are accountable for customer retention. Your product launch goals may include one or all of these metrics. Your goals could also include other common metrics such as growing product adoption, increasing monthly (or weekly, or daily) active users, or increasing the sales win-loss ratio.

Bottom-Line KPIs Are a Top Priority for Product Marketers

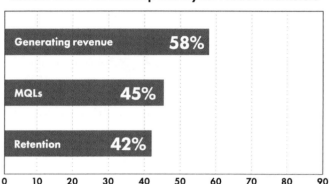

When thinking through goals, choose ones that will impact your business and align to the reasons why you're doing the launch in the first place. Here's a hint: It's more helpful to start with the goals and build out the GTM plan from that, rather than build the plan and tack on the goals at the end. This is discussed further in Part 5.

INTRODUCTION TO THE LAUNCH CHECKLIST

Meet the launch checklist—your new best friend (available on Productlaunch.pro). This is your organizational mainframe, your mission control, your GSD (get sh*t done) list. You should become obsessed with this list and make sure it is always up to date and meets the demands of the launch you are running. The checklist includes a list of each task that needs to be completed with the due date, status, owner, priority level, and a space for notes and links. The template is already prepopulated with several initiatives I've used in prior launches (mostly for B2B tech companies). Every company and product is different, so customize this to fit your needs. Managing this GTM plan where all stakeholders can track your progress is a great way to build alignment and confidence in the launch process.

> **LAUNCH LEARNING:** I prefer to use Google Sheets to easily keep shareholders in the loop with what's happening as well as to receive and respond to comments on the plan.

We'll cover the following sections in the launch checklist:

- Section 1: Strategic Readiness
- Section 2: External Promotion
- Section 3: Sales Enablement
- Section 4: Internal Launch Communications

After reviewing this section and the corresponding GTM template, I encourage you to brainstorm with your team to make sure you have every activity that makes sense for your business covered. This template is meant to get you started, but you know the ins and outs of your business and which channels will work best to get the launch information out to both your internal teams and customers.

The launch checklist:

Task	Due Date	Status	Responsible	Priority	Notes
Strategic Readiness/Positioning/Branding					
Establish key performance metrics and goals		Not Started	PM, Product Specialist	High	
Determine and document competitive landscape and positioning		Not Started	PMM	Medium	
Develop the message		Not Started	PMM	Low	
Develop RACI		In Progress	Product	High	
External Promotion					
Organic digital—SEO		Complete	Digital	High	
Press: Create strategy (reach out to friendlies, PR, etc.)		In Progress	PR		
In-product messaging for product releases		Not Started	Technical Writer (TBD)		
Content strategy (blogs, social)		Not Started	PMM		
Paid digital—SEM, display ads		In Progress	Digital		
Screengrabs/visuals of new product feature		In Progress	PM		
Add in to product spotlight (newsletter)		Complete	PMM		
In-product strategy		Complete	Growth		
Rollout product spotlight (in dash)		In Progress	Growth		
Blog post		In Progress	Content		

Section 1: Strategic Readiness

The first section, Strategic Readiness, makes sure you have everything ready to move forward with the launch from a strategic lens—the who, what, when, where, why, and how of the launch. These items form the strategic basis of your launch and should be taken care of first, and they are listed again on your sheet to make sure you've addressed them. Here are the key items:

- **(Who)**—Target market, defined specifically as possible, and personas, if available. Consider listing who is NOT part of the target audience.
  - » Determine and document competitive landscape and positioning.
- **(Who—internal)**—Internal stakeholders
- **(What)**—A review of what is launching, including product stage, new features, and specs.
  - » The messaging and positioning for your launch
- **(When) Launch milestones**—You've already listed these out on the first page
- **(Where) Channel plan**—Where are you launching and how will this be communicated?
- **(Why)**—Establish key performance metrics and goals.

Section 2: External Promotion
(External Channels)

External Promotion is all about where your target audience is going to see your message. This is really the bread and butter of your launch plan. The table below is a quick primer on some of the most popular types of external promotion. Think of this as a checklist where you can pick and choose the items that make the most sense for your business.

Channels for Promoting Your Launch

For more details, see the Appendix on the following page.

Channel	Reasons for using
Organic digital—search engine optimization (SEO)	This is a long-term, strategic initiative to target prospects and customers while they are actively searching for your brand or category.
Press—hire a PR agency or someone internal to pitch	You can use press for a major product launch or a company launch. Many startups think they can "email some reporters" to get press, but it's challenging to get a reporter to write about you without the help of skilled professionals.
Written case studies and testimonials	If you have clients who have already tried your product (i.e., beta testers) and who will speak for you, get them to! Ask for a simple quote (or write one and have them approve it) with their logo for something low key, or interview them and create a written case study with the content.
Video case study	Videos of customers singing your praises are extremely effective but can be very time intensive and expensive. You'll need help with the questions and maybe a script, and a professional videographer and editor.
Paid digital—search engine marketing (SEM), display ads, or video ads	If you're new to a market and your website is brand new, I highly recommend using paid ads. Doing it yourself can be time intensive but on the less expensive side, or you can hire someone.
In-product messaging for product releases	Use this to give existing customers a heads-up about a new product or feature. Tools like Pendo, Amplitude, and AppCues are great for product messaging on the fly.
Blogs and social posts	Blogs and social posts are great to drive awareness of your product and/or company online. They should be an ongoing staple of your marketing strategy because they help you build up SEO and create a reason to contact your customers. Hire a writer in-house or outsource this.
Content update for website	If you have an existing website, you should absolutely update the product content as part of your launch strategy. If you don't have a website, you can easily build out a basic one with tools like WordPress and Wix.
External email announcement	Emails should always be a staple of your product or company launch. Collect emails everywhere you can (legally!)—on your website, at events, etc., and always continue to build this list.
Update help center content	If you have a help center or knowledge base, it is a best practice to consistently update content once new features and products become available. This not only helps to promote your product but also makes sure customers can learn more about the "how to" and troubleshoot if needed.
Resellers	Companies often have relationships with resellers, which are companies that purchase goods or services with the intention of selling them rather than consuming or using them.
Channel partners	Often, companies employ channel partners, which work with a company to market and sell their services, technologies, or products. This often includes an element of co-branding, so listing these out in advance and knowing which materials you'll need for them is helpful for a launch.

Section 3: Sales Enablement (Internal Channels)

The third section, Sales Enablement, assumes you have a sales team or a customer-facing team such as customer service. Sales enablement is critical to any company with a sales team, account management teams, or customer service teams, as they are the front line to any customers and prospects. The goal of sales enablement is not only to educate the team to be able to speak credibly about the product but also to get the internal teams excited about the launch. Timing is key with sellers and customer service teams as you need them to be not only aware of the launch but trained on it before it goes live. Otherwise, they may lose credibility when speaking about it to clients and prospects. The most successful companies also use their sales team as advocates for their products. It is your job to teach them why they should love the product and to shout it from the rooftops!

The table below lists some items you may consider for your sales enablement activities. Ideally, all assets for sales will be available before the launch date. Remember, keep your sales team in the loop using whatever channels are available to you. If they don't know about a launch, that's on you!

Sales Enablement Channels

Sales enablement	Reasons for using
Product training	Product training is essential for any sales or customer service team to make sure they are fluent in the features and value of the new product and to make sure they aren't "caught off guard" with any customer questions.
Sales training	Sales training is a must-have to make sure the sellers understand both the what and the why of the new product or feature. Without this, salespeople will say whatever they want about the product.
Sales certification	If the product is complicated or changes the positioning of your company, consider doing a sales certification. Usually, this requires creating a pitch script and a rubric. Salespeople pitch and/or demo the product to leadership, and only when they "pass" can they sell it.
Talking points/ Pitch script	Talking points or a full pitch script can be valuable for more complicated products.
Product slides	Creating a few slides about the product is a quick way to get sales the info they need about a product and help them incorporate it into their existing pitch deck.
One sheet	Creating a high-quality one sheet to send to prospects and customers can be an effective follow-up for sales, but it is also time consuming. You need a well-designed template, high-quality screenshots, and the right messaging and positioning. Save this for your highest priority launches.
Comm doc/ Internal FAQ	This internal document is a must-have for any launch as it is your "single source of truth." If possible, work with the product manager (PM) on this document and always keep it updated with new product information and assets.
Announcements	Many companies have weekly all-hands meetings or sales meetings; this is a great way to make sure sales and other business units know the key dates and the high-level picture of your launch.
Goals/Incentives	Work with sales leadership to develop specific sales targets and related incentives around selling this specific product or feature. For example, you could offer a bonus for a particular target hit, or a fun spiff such as a trip or a gift.
Post materials to asset management system (intranet, Google Drive folder, etc.)	Make sure that whatever you create lives in the system that sales accesses regularly. If they don't have one, start a Google Drive or Dropbox folder with launch assets. I like to package all the assets for a launch and call them a "sales pack" to deliver to teams.

Section 4: Internal Launch Communications

Finally, no launch is complete without internal launch communications, the final section on the launch checklist tab. Do not skip this part! Even if your launch is perfect externally, if you miss on the internal communications, it doesn't matter. This section is where you make sure you're effectively communicating the launch to your colleagues.

I recommend thinking through all the various stakeholders, groups, and regions that need to know about the launch and when. Make that list and check it with other people on your team—are you missing anyone? Then think about the best way to communicate with them—is it via email, slides at their team meeting, at your company all-hands, via Slack, or all of the above? It's likely some combination of these and whatever approach you choose, it likely needs to be repeated. Communicate the message often and make it as entertaining as possible; you want your internal teams to remember the message of the launch and be as excited as the product team is about it. I have made launch announcements more fun with swag (gifts), quizzes on the content, "celebrity" guest appearances (i.e., executives), and once with a round of scotch for an evening sales leadership meeting where I was the last presenter.

Note that this section is organized by the timing leading up to the launch.

Internal Launch Communication Activities

Activity	Timing
Weekly update to key stakeholders	6–12 weeks before launch
Roadshow to top internal teams	2 weeks before launch
Company-wide communication with all dates, links, resources, and what to expect	1 week before launch
Day-of-launch email with all links, resources, and any early feedback (from social media, internal stake-holders, customers, or press)	Day of launch
Recap of activities, links to all documents, press, impact to goals	1 week post launch
Monthly recaps and reporting on adoption metrics	Post launch for 3–6 months

Optional: Post-Launch Momentum

"Rolling Thunder"

You've launched your product, had the party, wrote the recap, now you're done, right? Unfortunately, your work isn't done with the launch, and in some ways, it's only just the beginning of the journey if you have adoption and revenue goals to hit. Although the launch is the biggest opportunity to get in front of your target audience, you can repackage your content and communications to get in front of your audience again and again—I call this the "rolling thunder" approach. Don't wait to develop the rolling thunder plan until after the launch; rather, work on it and get approval from your stakeholders during the rest of the launch planning.

In the B2B (business-to-business) space, post-launch momentum can be accomplished in a number of ways. I'm a fan of creating a couple of core content pieces—for example, a white paper with new research or a deck employees can present in multiple contexts, and finding different ways to "slice and dice" it into blogs, social content, or emails. This enables you to give the content more "legs" and have more mini targeted moments to promote to your customer base.

These are the best ways to keep a product in the conversation post launch:

- **Research white paper**—Custom or compiled research with shareable stats. Bonus points if you can do this with an industry or analyst partner for added leverage (such as Gartner or Forrester).
- **Video**—Try showcasing clients, employees, or the product in a snappy video that encapsulates your key messages.
- **Customer events**—Do you have super-users who would love to hear more about your product? Invite them for a customer advisory board or user conference.
- **Customer case studies**—It's great to have case studies, but it's the promotion of those case studies that really matters. A customer speaking on your behalf on a webinar, at a conference, or on a podcast is a great way to keep the momentum.
- **Infographic**—Use the same stats as a research paper, just in a more visual form.
- **Webinar series**—Go top of the funnel to explore challenges or explain the product in more detail.

You get more legs on this if you can find an industry partner to pair with.

- **Direct mail**—Sounds crazy, but for anyone with bigger clients they are targeting, this can be a great channel. Don't just send a postcard, though; this needs to be something compelling that someone would want (cupcakes and cookies have been a hit!). This is also best paired with an email or larger account-based strategy to this group.

- **Digital marketing**—All of the above can be promoted with ads. Once you create your post-launch content, don't forget to market it!

MANAGING MULTIPLE LAUNCHES: TIERING, BUNDLING, AND PRODUCT STAGES

Some of you might be staring down a full calendar of dozens of launches over the next few months. How will you manage? Let me introduce you to your toolkit: tiering, bundling, and product stages. Tiering helps you define how "big" you want to go with a launch in relationship to others, bundling brings multiple related features together in a single launch, and product stages help you get on the same page with your product managers and customers by releasing a product with an alpha or beta designation.

Tiering

As you are thinking about how to go to market, it's important to decide how "big" you want to go with the product launch and the story you are trying to tell in market with the launch. A launch could be a huge game-changing product that affects millions of people, such as the iPhone, or it could be a feature update that improves the experience for a handful of users, such as a UI (user interface) update. Either way, you need to decide how big you want the launch to be, and one of the best ways to do this is with tiers.

Time, resources, and budget all come into play when defining the launch tiers. That's why I think "tiering" is such a good method to categorizing your launch moments, especially if you think you'll have more than one coming up. The way I like to think about tiering is numerically: Tiers 1, 2, and 3. You might have heard this expressed as T-shirt sizes—large, medium, and small—or even as precious metals—platinum, gold, or silver. The concept is the same throughout. In the numerical tiering structure, Tier 1 is the biggest launch you'll have in a quarter; Tier 2 launches are generally important to the sales teams and your core customers but not "game changing"; and Tier 3 launches are cosmetic updates or bug fixes, and you might have dozens of these a quarter. I often get asked why every launch isn't a Tier 1. The answer is, prioritization of resources and reception in the market. If everything you are releasing is treated the same as the iPhone, the market and your customers will become fatigued.

The tiers don't reflect the time and effort the product and engineering teams have put in (again, sometimes a company will work for months or years on back-end systems upgrades that you don't want to talk about publicly). The launch is meant to be an exciting moment to drive awareness of a product for a particular target market that will have some kind of result, usually a purchase of that product. This means you may occasionally need to push back against product or engineering teams that want to celebrate their achievements with a product launch.

Product Launch Tiers

Launch Tier	Impact	Timing
Tier 1 Launch	A product that is strategically important to the business that you want everyone, internally and externally, talking about. 1–2 max per quarter.	Go big with a client event, custom video content, press, and executive sponsorship internally.
Tier 2 Launch	A product or feature launch that will impact many customers. A handful per quarter.	"The basics"—a blog post, new web page, sales collateral.
Tier 3 Launch	Products or features that are mostly an upgrade or affect a small subset of customers. Potentially dozens per quarter.	A blog post announcement and an internal heads-up in the internal sales newsletter.

Bundling

If you have multiple smaller products and features that are similar, you may consider bundling launches with similar themes. This will help you create effective stories in market and make your launches appear bigger than they are. One approach is to look at your upcoming roadmap and try to bucket the features into similar themes—for example, faster insights or seamless integrations. Then bundle several features around that theme and even release them around an event you are having in market (e.g., a customer event, conference, etc.).

For example, one of my favorite launches was at a company called SocialChorus (now called Firstup), where I managed a bundled launch around 12 Tier 2 features that were technically out to market but hadn't received any promotion. They were all impactful for our core audience of communication professionals and differentiated us from the competition, but individually, it was challenging to have a big launch around it. We pulled them all together and billed the release as an "Innovation Lab" of all new and exciting features. The story was about how engineering and product had been hard at work, building all these different features that would help the communicator do their job better. And it was very well received. We got several trade press publications to report on the launch and won an award for the Best Product Launch at the Amplitude Amplify conference in 2018.

Product Stages

Understanding the stage your product or engineering team is in is critical. You usually wouldn't talk about a product publicly until it is at least in the beta phase. Until that point, you are testing if that product will even work and if it has "product/market" fit, or if it will be successful with your intended target market.

Product Stage Definition

Stage	Goals
Market validation / Discovery	• Establish a hypothesis of product/market fit (including target market) • Understand if the product is something we should pursue • Dive deep into the competitive landscape • *(Note: Not sharing with customers at this point)*
Alpha—Evaluation Stage	• Work closely with a handful of customers (fewer than 10) • Validate the initial concept • Iterate to a minimum viable product (MVP) • May decide not to pursue at this stage
Closed Beta-Testing with customers	• Start driving adoption through demand generation or selling efforts • Start selling into international markets • Iterate product to fit market needs • Test marketing messaging and provide sales collateral • Create KPIs/gates for moving to the next stage
Open Beta-Testing with customers through sales	• Sales is able to sell at their discretion • All marketing materials are available and localized • Self-serve UI being tested on a percentage of customers • Potential marketing push
General Availability (GA)—Full global launch	• Product is available for all customers

What to Do When Something Goes Wrong
(Hint: It Will)

Although I've managed over 250 launches, not even one has gone perfectly. "WHAT?" You might be thinking, "Why did I buy this book?" Before you write me an angry review, know that most of the time when something does go wrong, only the person running the launch or a small number of people internally actually know about it. The trick is understanding what could go wrong and catching any mistakes early.

At the end of the day, know that the likelihood of your launch going "perfectly" is about 0 percent. But it's okay, as the target customer is never the wiser. To help you mitigate your launch anxiety, here are some common things that can go wrong and how to prevent them.

What to Do When Something Goes Wrong

What could go wrong	How to prevent it	How to salvage
A team (or person) internally didn't know the launch was happening; they're furious	Build the RACI (Responsible, Accountable, Consulted, Informed), have it approved, and constantly ask others if anyone is missing.	Check to see if they were on the communications and point them to it if they were. If not, explain your process and how you may have missed them. Apologize, but don't grovel.
Some marketing materials aren't ready on time	Manage the GTM checklist and hold collaborators and vendors accountable.	Send out a list of what is finalized with all the links to assets. Give deadlines you can hit on the remaining pieces of collateral.
Your website updates didn't launch at the right time	Micromanage the day-of-launch checklist; make sure everyone knows exactly what they're doing at exactly what time.	What can I say, it happens! Try to get it up as soon as possible, find out what went wrong, and communicate a post-mortem.
The press team flubbed	Make sure they are buttoned up on timing and messaging well before the launch. Make sure there is one point of contact.	It really depends on how big of a flub. There are some things that are out of your control. If your external press team really dropped the ball somehow, it may be time to look elsewhere.
You sent the wrong email or package	Check everything twice. Before you press "send" on a large client or internal communication, make sure that someone who isn't sleep deprived from launch planning checks all your links, addresses, grammar, and other pertinent details.	At NextRoll, we once sent a "welcome" box to a group of prospective clients, not our new clients as intended. We sent a "we flubbed" email, and got a ton of great responses; we even got a high conversion rate on the accidental campaign.

TAKEAWAYS

This chapter was meant to get you organized and feeling confident for your first launch. In this section, you learned the importance of strategy, the fundamentals of a launch checklist, and some ideas for channels that you could be running to make your launch effective. Remember to download your free launch checklist at Productlaunch.pro. Some of the top takeaways to remember are:

- ✓ You might not always need a launch. Make sure you're asking the right questions before you jump into action.
- ✓ Set your launch strategy—everything else is dictated by that.
- ✓ Strategy is not only what you plan to do but also what you plan on NOT doing.
- ✓ Your launch plan is customizable to your business and your needs, but once it's set, keep it up to date.
- ✓ Tiering, bundling, and product stages are effective ways to manage many launches.

PART 2

KNOW YOUR TARGET MARKET (YOUR CUSTOMER)

"Don't find customers for your products.
Find products for your customers."

—**Seth Godin**, marketing guru, author, speaker

The scene: Glass-windowed conference room at an open-plan tech office in San Francisco. A dog is under the table; micro-kitchen snacks are scattered about; and the product manager, adorned in a company hoodie, just finished her presentation on the next new game-changing product. After the applause settles, one brave product marketer dares to ask, "So who is this product for?" The product manager retorts, as though it's painfully obvious, "Well, that's easy—it's for *everyone!*"

While applause continues and the CFO high-fives the presenter, the product marketer at the table is silently screaming, "NOOOOOOOOOOOOOOOOOOOO!!!"

"It's for everyone" may be the worst three words in the product marketer's lexicon. Why? Because if your product is for everyone, *it's actually for no one.* To kick off a product launch, it's extremely important to define who you are marketing to. This chapter will show you how.

IF YOUR PRODUCT IS FOR "EVERYONE," IT'S ACTUALLY FOR NO ONE

Both brand-new companies and established companies need to have a specific customer in mind for their product launches. If you don't have a defined customer in mind, how are you going to know the product is great for them? Furthermore, how will you be able to reach them? "For everyone" technically means people (or dogs, too? I mean, you did say everyone) in all countries, of all ages, with all technical capabilities, of all income levels...well, you get the idea. I even hear this in a business-to-business (B2B) context, and sometimes the product or engineering team STILL insists it's for everyone (my first question: don't they at least have to work at a business?).

If you say your product is "for everyone," what I hear is that you don't really know anything about your customer. At all. You haven't taken the time to speak to any customer or prospect, to research how they would use your product, why they would love it (or hate it), how you would tell them about new features. Instead, the "customers" are just an amorphous blob who should automatically fall in love with your product. It's sloppy.

I was once consulting for a series A company that had one hit product and was looking for the next winner. They brought me in to "productize" their existing technology to make the next product fit the customer base rather than looking at the challenges of the customer and building the product for those challenges. Your basic square peg, round hole scenario. It wasn't successful (neither my project nor the business ultimately). This is a classic mistake in tech—the "if we build it, they will come" ideology. The truth is, you're far more likely to find success by understanding the challenge a specific potential customer segment has and building something that will solve the problem for them. Try not to make the same mistake I once did: if you're being asked to find the product/market fit after the product or technology has been created, know that it's an uphill battle.

The Business Rationale for Knowing Your Customers: Product/Market Fit

Knowing your customers helps you understand your market size, or TAM (total addressable market), which includes how many customers could potentially use your product, the potential growth rate of those customers, and projected revenue. How can you scope out market size if your target is the entire world and everyone in it? How can you be sure that the feature set included is what this market needs? If your product is for "everyone," you can't.

If you don't understand your market, you won't be able to tell if there is a product/market fit because you don't know which market you're trying to tackle. In the PMARCA guide to startups, Marc Andreesen explains, "Product/market fit means being in a good market with a product that can satisfy that market." The guide goes on to explain, in bold, "The #1 company killer is lack of market." You have essentially failed before even launching unless you have figured out who your customer is.

LAUNCH LEARNING:

"Product/market fit means being in a good market with a product that can satisfy that market."

—Marc Andreesen

When You Don't Research Your Audience

When I was the Head of Product Marketing at AdRoll (now NextRoll), we made a catastrophic mistake related to understanding an audience when launching a new product, known as email retargeting. For some context, AdRoll at the time was primarily known for a type of digital marketing called retargeting, which is when you visit a web page and later see an ad promoting the same product (yes, those annoying ads that "follow you around" the internet, but man, are they effective!). This new product let customers retarget via email, which meant our system could send an automated email about a product a consumer had just viewed directly to them. We tested the alpha version of the product with a handful of clients, and it showed significant success, so we thought we were ready to release it to the world. When we did, it totally flopped.

What happened? We failed to see a critical distinction in how this product worked when we tested it with only a handful of clients. These clients were small and managed both the digital and email marketing for their companies. They could easily implement something like this using their same small teams and budget because they were able to count any sales toward their digital marketing ROI (return on investment). However, when we tried to sell into slightly bigger clients, we couldn't get any traction. We didn't realize that their email marketing and digital marketing teams were not as connected as we originally thought. In fact, the email marketing team wanted *nothing* to do with the digital marketing team sending what they thought of as "random" emails on top of their carefully curated email plans. And the digital marketing team didn't want to pay more in advertising fees to give the email marketing team "free" conversions that could have otherwise been attributed to their digital marketing efforts, as that last touch or purchase would be attributed to email. Neither team at these bigger companies wanted to touch the product.

I wish we would have done two things differently. First, I wish we would have made sure our early testing included businesses of all sizes and thoroughly interviewing the many teams involved. Second, I wish we would have changed our GTM strategy and targeted the head of marketing, which straddled both the digital and email marketing teams, instead of the individual teams. Then they could have helped us break down the siloes of reporting and budget and help us navigate how to get this ROI-positive product in their hands. However, as is the fate of so many products, this one didn't succeed, and we quickly pulled it out of our product offering.

Why Is This Important for a Product Launch?

You need to understand your potential customer before you bring a product to market, as this is a major part of your GTM strategy. This will help you dictate who to target, how to target them (which channels), and even what you say (the messaging). Think about it: if your product was targeting a small owner of a mom-and-pop shop, compared to a CMO at a *Fortune* 500 company, you would go about your launch strategy differently. This may seem obvious, but ask the dumb question if you're not sure who the product is for—it's highly probable no one else has.

LAUNCH LEARNING: Ask the "dumb question" if you're not sure—"who is this product for?"

Similarly, make sure you know if this product is for new or existing customers, and if there are any characteristics to segment them even further. A major marketer's dilemma is making sure that they are marketing to the right group with the right messaging, and the further you can segment this, the better.

It's also important to understand the audience for the nuances of the launch. If you already have a customer base, are you launching this product to all your customers around the world at one time? For larger businesses and those with a global reach, this can add weeks to your timeline if you're trying to launch all at once (coordination with global teams and translations alone can add several weeks). It's perfectly acceptable to stagger launches—that is, launch in the United

States first, followed by English-speaking countries outside of the United States, then finally globally. This helps you get a better handle on timing, and I provide an example of this in the "Nail the Launch Timing" chapter of this book.

HOW TO TALK TO YOUR CUSTOMERS

Talking to customers or prospective customers is often the most overlooked part of a GTM strategy. It blows me away every time I hear that people have not talked to customers before developing or launching a product. Ideally, if you're working with a product manager, they will have customers that are alpha or beta testing a product or throughout the product life cycle (see Product Stages section in Part 1 for more details). Betas are a great time to piggyback on the conversations the product manager is already having to make sure product messaging will work and that there is indeed a product/market fit.

Talking to customers can also help you plan your marketing activities—understanding where they go for information today and how they would like to see the information presented (for more, review some of the ideas in the External Promotion section in Part 1).

6 WAYS TO QUICKLY DEFINE
YOUR CUSTOMERS

Whether you have a customer base already with other products or are launching a new product to a new market completely, the following are some ways to help define who your customers are:

1. Develop a hypothesis of who would use your product. If you do not have any customers using the product yet, make an educated guess by speaking to those who worked on the product about the challenges it solves. Try to be as specific as possible. For example: Northern California mothers who strive to be conscientious consumers and want to avoid plastic packaging.

2. Look at competitors to your product: Who are they marketing to? What are they saying? Is this the same or different for your product? Why? Are there any "blank spaces"? Picking a market your competitors are not in can be a way to differentiate yourself from the competition. For example, if you have many competitors in the enterprise space, consider going for small and medium businesses.

3. Talk to people who are in your hypothesized customer base. Yes, *real people*. And yes, *you*, not some outside research firm that hands you a nice PowerPoint. You need to hear their language and see with your own eyes if their challenges are ones you can solve. Here are a few ways you can learn more about your potential customers:

   a. Hold focus groups online

   b. Run surveys—e.g., on LinkedIn and Facebook or with more established, random sampling tools like Qualtrics offers

   c. Interview your customers for an incentive

   d. Connect with your potential customers at conferences (virtual or otherwise)

   e. Find potential customers online with ads on LinkedIn or through Vancery (a research participant finder firm)

   f. Sit in on conversations with beta testers that the product managers or UX team is hosting

   g. Look at online forums for the kinds of conversations your potential customers have (e.g., subreddits for specific topics on Reddit)

4. Once you find them, ask everyone you talk to the same basic questions and record the audio (with

their permission) or take diligent notes. Here are some basic questions (a more built-out script appears later in the chapter).

   a. What are your challenges?

   b. What kinds of solutions do you use today?

   c. How happy are you with the alternative?

   d. What features are "must-haves"?

5. After all of this, if you still have no idea, ask yourself if launching this product is worth your time.

6. If you have more than one type of customer, that's okay. Different groups of customers are known as segments, and you can have slightly different messaging, marketing, and promotion to each of these.

LAUNCH LEARNING: No matter what approach you take to get to know your customers, put a plan together, get buy-in from stakeholders, and communicate the results.

Customer Interviews

At AdRoll (now NextRoll), I was tasked with a large project to segment our customers and develop revised GTM plans for each segment. However, we had a problem: we didn't *really* know who our customers were. Sure, we knew their titles, companies, and what they spent with us, but we had no clue what really made them tick or why they bought from us versus the competition.

I decided to embark on a motivation-driven interview project by interviewing 30 people: some current customers, some prospects, and some churned (no-longer-active customers). I gave each a $50 Amazon gift card for their time. The interviews were based on the Jobs to Be Done methodology (see example to come), created by the former Harvard Business School professor Clayton Christensen. Tactically, I wrote up a script, trained my team on the interviews, and had them all record their interactions (I led about 5 myself). I then had them fill in the key responses on a spreadsheet and coded all of the responses. I personally listened to all 30 interview recordings and added to the spreadsheet as I discovered new insights.

The interviews helped us discern patterns to help us segment to the size of their marketing team, which is different than how we were looking at customers previously (by industry and dollar amount they spent with us). We realized with these new segments, each had different motivations for buying, and we should change our GTM strategy to better reach these customers.

To make sure this new approach worked, I then used a survey to test new segment-specific messaging to a larger group of customers by creating four mock home pages with different taglines and asking people to rank their favorites and why. For the incentive, I held a contest in which one winner would receive a $250 Amazon gift card. The results were illuminating, and we got enough responses in three days to be able to make an informed decision about a new messaging strategy.

TACTICS FOR QUICK, SCRAPPY RESEARCH

Once you've defined your audience, you need to understand a little bit more about what makes them "tick." This helps with marketing messaging, where to promote, as well as future product development.

Here are some "quick win" ways to get great and quick customer research without breaking your budget.

Tactic 1: Email Surveys

The quickest way to get the most respondents for a research study is to tap into your existing email list and send out a survey. Try segmenting your email lists in a way that makes the most sense. For example, you might send different emails to each group of current, churned, or prospective customers.

Many companies are nervous to do this because they don't want to bombard their customer base with another email, but planning ahead and finding an appropriate time to slot this in can go a long way. I recommend TypeForm for creating quick surveys because they also make it easy to see the results in real time. Make the survey more enticing by offering an incentive (see more on that later) and keeping it really short and sweet.

Tactic 2: Phone Interviews

If you have the bandwidth and want to go deeper, 30-minute interviews with at least 5 customers can go a long way. Any less than 5 and you risk leaning too heavily on one individual respondent's opinions. The trick with interviews is to develop a script and to ask every customer the same set of questions. Then, when you are looking at all the answers on a spreadsheet, you can review them as a collective rather than as individual responses and find patterns.

The biggest pain for interviews is the scheduling. I recommend sending out an email (to a similar list as your survey list) and including a bookable button from a free service such as Calendly. This site allows you to set the time zones and times that work for you and lets people book directly on your calendar.

To take the call, try Dialpad Meetings, formerly Uber-Conference, another service with a free trial that lets you dial in by phone or online and also allows you to record the call. Absolutely make sure you ask for permission before recording the call; it is illegal in some places (like California) to record without someone's consent.

If you need to show any product/UI/design mocks or have a person walk through an interface as part of your study, send them a link in advance and use a program like Google Hangouts or Zoom to share your screen.

> **LAUNCH LEARNING:** There is a lot of value from personally running the interviews or at least listening to recordings. You can note down specific words they use for future messaging, moments of hesitation, or moments of excitement. Be close to this part of the research.

Tactic 3: iPad Surveys at a Conference

If you want to be scrappy, try bringing an iPad with a pre-loaded survey to a conference. This is a great way to get a lot of responses from your target audience (assuming the conference is geared toward this audience). This is also a good way to strike up conversations with prospective clients. Again, I like to use Google Forms for this. You can set up at a booth or just walk around asking people to take your survey for $5. (Then hand them a crisp $5 or a Starbucks card—the instant gratification makes people's day!). At one point doing this recently, I had a line of people wanting to see what all the fuss was about...and how to get their $5! You could offer the same type of experience with virtual booths, promotions, and sending a $5 gift card via email.

Tactic 4: LinkedIn Messages

LinkedIn advertising can be a great channel for getting quick responses, either for surveys or to recruit for an interview. The great thing about this is it allows you to target your perfect audience. Try different headlines, such as leading with an incentive, to see what your best response rate is.

Tactic 5: Recruit Interviewees Using a Recruitment Tool Like Vancery

Vancery allows you to target specific professionals to take surveys and/or set up customer/prospect interviews. You can target by region, profession, and even role to recruit for a particular project. Note that this approach can be on the pricier side as recruiting certain roles might cost more than $100 per respondent for their time. It is quick, however, and the insights are well worth the price.

Tactic 6: Incentivize

It would be great if everyone would commit to your awesome research project out of the goodness of their hearts, but the reality is that people are busy and they want their time to be worth something. For quick surveys, I recommend these approaches for incentives:

- Something small like a $5 or $10 Amazon gift card
- A small credit or discount to your business
- A donation to a charity
- A raffle—with either a larger monetary incentive ($250–$500) or something cool (the latest iPad, a chance to have lunch with your CEO—whatever you think your audience will care about).

IMPORTANT QUESTIONS TO ASK YOUR CUSTOMERS

To understand what makes your potential target customers tick, below are some specific questions that you can ask them. These questions are adapted from former Harvard Business School professor Clayton Christensen's theory of Jobs to Be Done. The premise of Jobs to Be Done is that you "hire" someone (or a company or a product) to do a specific job for you, and sometimes it isn't what you expected. You can look at the questions here or download a copy at Productlaunch.pro.

JOBS TO BE DONE SCRIPT

Basic questions (you can figure these out usually with LinkedIn):

- What company are you at?
- What position do you hold?
- How long have you been there?
- What types of responsibilities do you have?

When researching a specific product, go back to the moment of purchase to understand the decision-making process and all the players involved:

- When did you first start using XYZ product?
- Who was involved in looking for a solution at the time?
- Who was involved in the final decision?
- What steps did everyone involved take to determine this was right for you/your company?

Try to find out more about the first thought about the purchase. Note all significant moments along the way.

- What was the first time you thought, "I need a new solution"?
- What made you think that? (Probe here.)
- What problem were you hoping to solve? What was the end game?
- Describe how budget decisions were made for this product (at home or at a business).
- Tell me about the (old solution).
  - » Can you remember how well that was working?
- What were the pain points of the new solution?

Build the consideration set:

The consideration set involves the time in which a person or company is looking at all the possible solutions for a job they want to fulfill through a product.

- Did you try other solutions to your problem? What kind of solutions were they?
- Did you look at or try out other products? Which ones?
- What were the things you were evaluating that were important to your decision?

- Why did you ultimately decide to buy the product you use today?
- What makes this product different from others you were considering?
- Was this a necessity or a nice-to-have?
- How painful was trying to find a solution on a scale from 1 to 10?
  » How painful was the alternative solutions?
- Please describe your experience with the product so far.

TAKEAWAYS

I hope by now it's become clear that understanding your customer (your market) is everything. Here are some ways you can make sure you truly understand your market before you build your strategy:

- ✓ Build your product for your customers' challenges, not the other way around.
- ✓ Ask the "dumb question" if you're not sure— "who is this product for?"

✓ There are many ways to approach customer research. No matter what tactics you choose, align with stakeholders and share the results.

✓ Research the group that you are going to be selling to—in and out. Make sure you understand their budgeting process, buying process, and everything in between.

✓ Understanding your customers can help you define your GTM strategy better and ultimately have a better launch because you're able to define who to target, how to target them (which channels), and even what you say (the messaging).

✓ Personally talk to the customers you think will be in your target market (yes, you, not someone else).

PART 3

ALIGN THE TEAM AND INTERNAL COMMUNICATION

"I look for people who have a slightly different perspective and are trying to move the needle a little bit and push boundaries."

—**Gwyneth Paltrow**, Founder and Chief Executive Officer, Goop.com

Product marketing sits at the intersection of sales, marketing, and product, and communicating with many stakeholders is not only part of the day-to-day job but critical to the success of a product launch. This is an exciting part of the job but also one of the hardest, as it necessitates a high level of communication and collaboration to get it right.

The Many Stakeholders of PMM

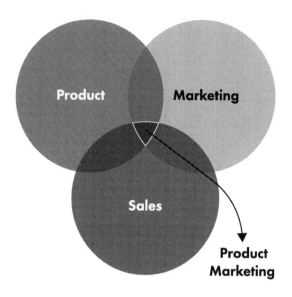

The best way to ensure you have a great launch is to make sure you have the right team and a communication game plan for how everyone will stay informed. This section will help you master the art of getting the right people on your team, championing your launch, and making sure everyone knows the important details.

ALIGNING THE TEAM

In a previous role, one of the first launches I worked on was major for our company, a redesigned campaign interface for our customers that would make them more effective at their jobs. The promise of the product was amazing, and initially everyone was very excited about it. Maybe too excited, since executives had already been talking about it publicly before launch and sharing it with customers before it was ready to ship. Let's just say that by the time I joined the project, bridges had already been burned internally. The launch date had slipped multiple times, making for a stressed-out product and engineering team and an irate sales team. It was clear a product marketer needed to right the ship.

I started to join our twice-weekly product launch meetings and realized quickly there was a major internal misalignment on the basics of the launch, including what features were launching and when. I set to work trying to understand the features that would launch on a realistic time frame and proposed a launch schedule that included a beta rollout with a GA (general availability) release about six months later. Once I got this approved by upper management, I set to work mending the communication issues that had plagued the project.

At an all-hands meeting in front of 500 colleagues, I shared the new plan in tandem with our director of product management to show that we were now aligned. The new plan also included an acknowledgment of the frustration of the slipped launch date. We had discovered through some internal focus groups that most people thought the launch was "just" an interface refresh, when it was, in reality, an entire rewrite of our back-end code base (read: a lot of work and super hard). During this all-hands, we shared an "under the hood" view of the technology to explain why it was taking longer than the sales team thought it should. We used the analogy that we were "working on a jet plane engine while the jet is already flying" (complete with a slide with an image of a jet!) to stress the point that this was no easy task—we were updating our most heavily used product, and downtime was not a possibility.

Once everyone was on the same page, we shared the razzle dazzle of the launch—how we would release it at our annual marketing event with key customers sharing their experiences, complete with a full sales kit with new decks, demo scripts, one sheets, and stats. After that meeting, it felt like we were one organization after the same goals, rather than disparate teams. We kept communication of progress on a monthly basis and made sure members of upper management were regularly communicating about this launch to their teams. In the end, we hit our new launch date, and we could all celebrate the success together.

Define Roles and Responsibilities Using the RACI Model

You may have heard this acronym in other contexts, but the RACI is incredibly important when it comes to having a successful GTM plan. RACI stands for "responsible, accountable, consulted, and informed" and it outlines your contributors and stakeholders. Defining the RACI for your project is essential to understanding who is doing the work, when everything is due, and who you should keep in the loop. You can have a RACI for each deliverable on your GTM plan, or just for each larger milestone. The basic premise is as follows and a person cannot appear in more than one bucket. You might have a RACI for your product overall, and you might have a RACI for the launch. I always keep an updated list of the RACI on my GTM tracker. I give some specific examples of RACI groups that have worked well for me in the "Nail the Launch Timing" section.

As you are selecting your team and building out the RACI, I encourage you to select as diverse a group as possible. Look for people who have different backgrounds and who are as representative of a group as possible to the broader population, including age, race, and gender. We've heard the stats and know that better decisions are made with more diverse groups, so be the leader of this change for your projects whenever possible.

The RACI Model

R	Responsible	The person doing the work
A	Accountable	The manager or executive sponsor, ultimately held accountable for the outcome
C	Consulted	Someone whose opinion you want to make sure you get, i.e., the content area expert
I	Informed	Anyone in the business who should be kept in the loop

LAUNCH LEARNING: As the launch leader, you can be the agent of change to select as diverse a group as possible for your launch team.

COMMUNICATE ABOUT YOUR PRODUCT INTERNALLY—"10-PERCENT TIME"

If you're at a larger company and launching a product, one of your biggest challenges might be getting people internally to care. You may hear this called battling for internal mindshare. Even if you're at a small startup, there is usually so much going on that it's a best practice to make sure the message is received by your colleagues. I think this is even more critical in remote working environments when we're on screens most of the day—people tend to have what I call goldfish memory. It's your job to remind them of this upcoming launch!

I have always encouraged my team to communicate regularly internally—I call this 10-percent time. This means quite literally that 10 percent of your time should be spent telling other people what you're doing. It sounds kind of self-promotional, but if the launch isn't a hit internally, it's going to be really hard to get the traction you need externally. You can think of internal promotion as building the case for marketing budget and resources. Additionally, it is great for your own visibility and personal growth if everyone at the company knows about your launch. Here are some ways to increase the visibility of your launch:

✓ Just because you've said it once, don't assume anyone heard you! Keep sharing launch updates in multiple channels. Try Slack, email, your company all-hands meetings, pod stand-up meetings, posters —anywhere that your internal audience might see the message.

✓ Remember to keep the message relevant: Why should they care? How will it affect them? Why is this exciting?

✓ Are there any stats you can reference that will make even the busiest executives perk up?

✓ Are there any internal case studies or stories you can share? Those tend to be a lot stickier. As an example, get a salesperson who participated in the beta to speak for you about what the product and pitch did for them.

> **LAUNCH LEARNING:** Ten percent of your time should be spent communicating about your launch internally.

Define the Right Internal Communication Channels

Not only is the right stakeholder group key, but defining your broader internal communication channels will make or break your launch. Is your company all about Slack? Is email king? Do PowerPoint presentations get respect? Perhaps it's all three. Here are some ideas for how to communicate the launch happenings and align your organization:

- The GTM checklist, updated at least weekly. Share with every communication.
- Regular email recaps with progress updates, charts, links, and next steps.
- Launch-specific Slack channel and updating on other relevant channels.
- Executive decks for monthly executive check-ins on launch progress.
- "Roadshow" deck to all teams you interface with (e.g., sales, marketing, regional teams, even engineering).

- Frequent presentations at all-hands meetings.
- Launch email once the product has launched.

Here is a real example of a launch email of a startup I founded with a few friends. (RIP, Phynder! The launch was great, but the company ultimately didn't make it). Notice how this communication clearly explains what the product is and how to access it and includes some visual elements as well.

Hi, friends and family,

Over the past year, some friends and I have been working on a new app that helps you buy and sell items locally—*it's called Phynder* (pronounced like Finder). We're excited to announce that the app is available for free on the Apple Store and launching in our first two markets—San Francisco and NYC!

What is Phynder?

The best way to describe Phynder is imagining if Craigslist and Tinder had a baby.

You can buy and sell anything locally—just like with Craigslist —but via an intuitive swipe-based mobile app that connects directly with Facebook and Venmo. This provides a more convenient and safe way to buy and sell locally.

Our team of 5 friends—a mix of UCSB, LMU, and UNF alums—have had a lot of fun designing and developing Phynder. And now we're looking to our networks of friends and family to help us with the beta test phase and to spread the word!

Here's how you can help:

- Share—Take a moment to follow us on Facebook. Please share any posts that will help spread the word. Even if you can't download the app, have an Android, or are not in NY or SF, we'd love it if you spread the word!
- Download and rate the app—Anyone can download the app on iPhone today, but it will only work in SF

and NYC within a 15-mile radius of the city center points until we roll it out to other cities in 2015 (we're looking at LA and Austin next). We are laser focused on creating the best user experience possible, so we are starting small to make sure we can do just that before expanding. The Android version will also be released as we grow.

- Upload items to sell—The more items we have in the marketplace, the better the user experience is for everyone. If you have things to sell, please post them today! If you're in the San Francisco area, we also have a dedicated team member who will help take photos of your items—send us an email at contact@phynder.com to get started.
- Feedback—We'd love to hear any feedback— suggestions, bugs, or anything. Please email us at contact@phynder.com.

Here are some things we're already selling to date:

- Guitars
- Hammocks
- Kid stuff
- Beach chairs
- And more!

Thanks for your support!

The Phynder team

Sam, Brian, Mary, Bryan, and Tim

In the final chapter, I share some specific examples of internal channels that worked for me for a successful launch.

> **LAUNCH LEARNING:** Use the best internal communication channels for your launch updates, and make the message sticky and exciting!

ALIGN PRODUCT MARKETING AND PRODUCT MANAGEMENT

It's a highly underrated concept that product marketers and product managers need to work together for a successful launch. Too many times, product marketers are not in the loop with launch goals, timelines, or customer research and are handed the information 2 weeks before launch and expected to be successful. A highly collaborative PMM and PM team can make the difference between a product launch that flops and one that rocks. Here are some of the best ways to ensure your teams have high communication so nothing is missed. I've focused on PMs and PMMs for the following advice, but this could relate to any of the members of the launch team you need to work with to be successful.

> **LAUNCH LEARNING:** The most successful product marketers become partners with product management teams, not "order takers."

1. Connect Teams Organically

Find a way for your teams to stay connected without adding more work. For example, you could try having product marketers and product managers sit together for at least half of each day—attending daily stand-ups, participating in sprint planning meetings, and having spontaneous conversations. By physically sitting together, product marketers and product managers become part of the same team at the early stages of product development. If your teams are remote or even in different time zones, find a way for them to connect such as video conferencing, holding regular stand-ups, or creating a shared Slack channel.

2. Create Shared Goals

It's hard to call a project successful—or unsuccessful—without defining clear goals at the outset. The most successful teams set their goals together. Early in the planning process, each team should make time to illustrate and understand their respective goals. Goals may include product adoption, beta sign-ups, or revenue growth, and progress should be tracked on a regular basis.

3. Be Each Other's Content-Area Experts

Product managers and marketers are experts in their domains and will find it beneficial to consult with each other on decisions both big and small. For example, product marketers should ask product managers to review positioning for additional industry and customer insights. In the same vein, product managers should ask product marketers to go through the customer experience of a new feature.

If you can, sit in the same room or at least on a video conference to review this type of information; it will be much richer than via email or document comments.

4. Share Customer Feedback

Both teams should talk to customers regularly but for different reasons. It's important for both teams to share customer insights and feedback with each other to inform product development and marketing messages. Product teams are often running user experience and demo feedback sessions; make sure you sit in on these sessions or get their results.

To get richer customer feedback and to understand customer motivations, I recommend surveying or interviewing 25 or so customers or prospects. This goes for both B2B and B2C. Talking to existing and, even better, churned customers will give you more insights (see Part 2 for more). Some questions to ask to uncover motivations:

- What were the real pain points they had that led them to buy your product?
- What were the alternatives to your product?

- How did they/would they get budget to buy your product?

5. Share and Celebrate Wins

Finally, when a goal is achieved, no matter how small, take time to pause and celebrate with everyone involved. Even a virtual high-five can go a long way. After all, when two teams work together, each victory is twice as sweet.

TAKEAWAYS

To have a successful launch, you need 2 things internally: the right team and a communication game plan for how everyone will stay informed.

- ✓ Be really specific about roles and responsibilities: responsible, accountable, consulted, and informed.
- ✓ People have goldfish memory—10% of your time should be spent communicating about your product internally.
- ✓ Use the best internal communication channels for your launch updates, and make the message sticky and exciting!

✓ Find ways to connect product marketing and product management, formally and informally, to ensure the success of a launch.

PART 4

PRIME THE POSITIONING AND MESSAGING

"Context enables people to figure out what's important. Positioning products is a lot like context setting in the opening of a movie."

—**April Dunford**, author of *Obviously Awesome*

According to The Product Marketing Alliance *State of Product Marketing 2020* report, the number one responsibility of a product marketer is the positioning and messaging of their products.

However, I frequently see the same issue: companies spend a mint on their website design, but it's extremely difficult to understand what the product does or why you (or anyone) would want to buy it. Why does this happen? Often, positioning and messaging are the last things a company thinks about after building a new product when they should occur in parallel to the product build and include input from the product management team. Your job owning the launch is to help potential customers quickly understand not only what your product does but also what the value is to them.

> **LAUNCH LEARNING:** Product positioning should be done in parallel to the product development, not after the fact.

This chapter will help you understand the difference between positioning and messaging and how both apply to your launch.

POSITIONING VERSUS MESSAGING

What's the Difference?

Often, the terms *positioning* and *messaging* are used interchangeably, but they are two distinct steps to share the value of a product to its intended audience. Positioning should come first, and only once that is agreed on should you work on the messaging. Here is an easy way to think about both concepts.

Positioning: The perception of your product in a customer's or prospect's mind. Although similar to a value proposition statement (which is broader in scope), the positioning statement homes in on exactly what makes your product different or special compared to the competition. A positioning statement is an internal, differentiated statement about your product, meant to be the North Star for all messaging. Usually, the positioning lives on an internal-only document that is shared only with those giving feedback on its development.

Messaging: External messaging framework relaying how your product is the best for your target audience. Messaging usually includes product benefits, features, or USPs (unique selling points). Note that messaging is then turned into *copy* (ideally, you hire a professional copywriter for this), which can be found on a website, product sheet, or anywhere your internal or external audience will see information about your product. Why would you hire a professional writer to develop copy from the messaging? Unless you have a writing background, this is often a different skillset required. A great writer can bring the messaging to life across many different channels, while still conveying the main points.

The goal of a product marketer or owner of the product launch is to create a solid positioning statement and messaging that can be translated by a copywriter to any type of medium: advertisements, websites, sales decks, or any other launch assets. I like to build this out using a positioning and messaging house, with the positioning statement as the roof and the messaging statements below, like 3 pillars holding it up.

The positioning and messaging house looks like this:

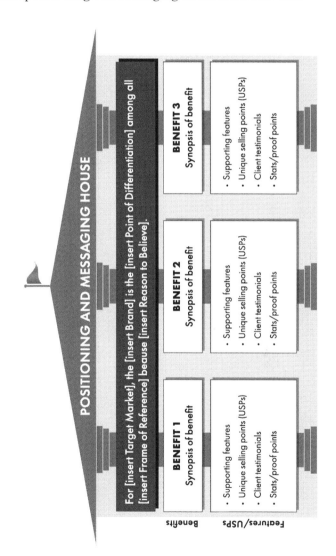

Head to Productlaunch.pro to download a copy of the positioning and messaging house.

Positioning

The positioning of a product is the perception of the product, relative to the competition, in a prospect's or customer's mind. This is the top of the messaging house, as it flows into everything else you will create. A key piece of the positioning statement is what makes your company different, *not just better*. The important thing about a differentiator is it allows your prospect to understand what makes you unique and to think of you in that context.

Creating effective positioning is a little bit art and a little bit science. The best example to understand positioning is the auto industry. Take Mercedes. When you think of a Mercedes, what comes to mind? Is it luxury and high class? What about a Subaru? Is it safety and adventure? Note that the associations are extremely different from each other. The brand associations you have are not accidental. They have been carefully constructed over the years through positioning to differentiate them from other cars in the market. The positioning is then heavily reinforced with messaging and other brand elements like visuals (commercials, print ads, etc.). You might not have the budget of a car company, but you still need to think about how you want your product to be perceived in the minds of your prospects.

A typical positioning statement framework looks like this:

For [Target Market], the [Brand or Product] is the [Point of Differentiation] among all [Frame of Reference/Category] because [Reason to Believe/Proof point].

Example positioning statement:

> For women road cyclists in Northern California, West Coast Cyclists offers the most comprehensive service among all cyclist shops because of their roadside assistance, bike maintenance training, and a 1-hour call-back guarantee.

This positioning statement works for two reasons: (1) They have differentiated by the market, women cyclists, which aren't commonly served specifically by the road cycling industry (shout-out to any other lady cyclists out there!). (2) They offer a point of differentiation, comprehensive service, which is different than any other company out there (or at least any that I know of). Armed with this statement, you could then create a differentiation strategy to target women with this unique point of differentiation.

Here's a breakdown of what each element of the positioning statement means:

- **Target market**—In the example, the target market is women road cyclists in Northern California. This is your ideal customer. Be as specific as possible here! Ask yourself some questions to specify even further, such as: Are these small, medium, or large enterprise businesses? Are your ideal customers male or female? Where do they live? What is their behavior? What motivates them?
- **Brand or product**—This one is easy—it's your brand or product. In the example, this is the fictitious company West Coast Cyclists.
- **Point of differentiation**—This is what makes you different or unique. In the example, it's the point about the shop being the most comprehensive service for cyclists. As discussed before, differentiation is incredibly important in marketing to make you stand out among the competition and not be commoditized.

- **Frame of reference**—This is also known as the "category" you're in, what a group of companies similar to yours will be called. In the example, it is cycling retailers. Many companies want to create a new category, but it's far easier for customers to understand what you do if you can relate it back to something that already exists.

- **Reason to believe/proof point**—This is a compelling feature, customer quote, or data point that reaffirms your main differentiation point. In the example, I used roadside assistance, bike maintenance training, and 1-hour call-back guarantee, both service features that level up to the main differentiation point of "fastest service." If you do not have something that fits here, ask yourself what you would need to get there or if you chose the right differentiation point.

You may notice that the statement I've come up with, and likely the one you've come up with for your own company, is rather clunky. It's meant to be internal, not something you would list on the homepage of your website. But once you have this in place, you can fine-tune and develop the messaging with the right frame of mind.

Messaging

Messaging refers to anything that is written about your product or company, internally and externally. It is often reinforced with other brand elements like visuals (pictures, infographics, videos, etc.). Messaging should also include the actual words your clients or prospects would use and avoid jargon as much as possible. Messaging is translated into copy by a writer and can appear in a number of different places, including:

- Every page of your website
- Sales decks, sales talking points, and pitch scripts
- Email campaigns
- White papers
- Webinars
- Speeches/speaking events
- Posters
- Packaging/labels
- Advertisements including the voice-over on audio ads

Thinking back to our messaging house, the messaging makes up the pillars, which hold up the roof of the positioning statements. The goal here is to create 3–5 benefit statements and lists of supporting features and unique selling points (USPs). A great way to develop the messaging for a product is to take a step back and review the market problems the product is solving.

I usually whiteboard a quick 3-column view like this with the product manager:

Market Problems	Problem-Solving Benefit Statement	Specific Features That Solve the Problem
The specific problems that your persona faced that led your team to develop the solution (see Part 1 for understanding the customer and their pain points). These usually do not appear in the messaging itself but help to frame your thinking.	In a few words, how does the product or feature solve the problem at hand? These statements can easily be turned into the 3–5 benefit pillars.	How does the product solve this problem? Are any of the features unique or differentiated? Put a star by these. These lists will become the support of the benefit statements.

This approach helps structure the benefits in a way that resonates with the copywriter. Here's an example of the messaging benefits you might come up with for West Coast Cyclists. Notice not all of them are differentiated (i.e., the last one could be any cycling shop; that's okay).

	Benefit 1	Benefit 2	Benefit 3
Messaging Pillar	The most comprehensive and trusted cycling service	For women cyclists, by women cyclists	Largest selection of bikes and bike equipment
Feature/USP	• Award-winning roadside assistance • Bike maintenance training to teach skills like fixing a flat tire	• Founded by women cyclists • 90 percent of customers are women • Bikes, seats, and apparel specially designed for women	• Largest selection of new and used road bikes in Northern California • State-of-the-art helmets, racks and other accessories

Putting this all together, here's what your messaging house would look like with all of the above incorporated. This is a document you could then use to get buy-in from everyone needed for the launch.

POSITIONING AND MESSAGING HOUSE

For road cyclists in Northern California, West Coast Cyclists offers the fastest service among all cyclist shops because of their roadside assistance and 1-hour call back guarantee.

Benefits

The most comprehensive and trusted cycling service	For women cyclists, by women cyclists	Largest selection of bikes and bike equipment

Features/USPs

• Award-winning roadside assistance • Maintenance training to teach skills like fixing a flat tire • 1-hour call back guarantee	• Founded by women cyclists • 90% of customers are women • Bikes, seats, and apparel specially designed for women	• Largest selection of new and used road bikes in California • State-of-the-art helmets, racks, and other accessories • Female-friendly bike attire

To turn this messaging into copy you would be comfortable with clients viewing, for each type of medium you are working on, think about the audience who will consume it. For the home page, for example, you want something short and punchy to catch a prospect's attention. For the sales pitch scripts, you have the runway to have much longer copy and be more explanatory. The important thing is that everything levels up to the positioning and messaging house and that no part of the messaging has gone rogue. Therefore, you only really need to get stakeholder feedback on the positioning and messaging house and do not need to ask them to review each part of the copy, which can be time consuming (I recommend you get approval on this first from stakeholders so there are no surprises, but in my experience, you want the CEO reviewing your positioning statement, not the copy on a one sheet). It's a great use of budget to employ a copywriter to transform your positioning into a messaging reality.

> **LAUNCH LEARNING:** Seek approval from executives
> (or the most senior people involved in your launch) on the
> positioning and messaging only. Let them know that once
> this is agreed on, the copy will be developed directly
> from these assets, but you don't want to burden them with
> reviewing every deliverable.

WHY DIFFERENTIATION IN POSITIONING AND MESSAGING MATTERS

Just as you need a deep understanding of your customers to build and market your products effectively, you also need to understand the competition so you can differentiate from them. Differentiating isn't just about being the best, fastest, or cheapest option; it's about being tangibly different enough from the competition so customers know why they should choose your brand and your brand alone over the competition.

Let's go deeper on an exercise mentioned previously. Take a moment to jot down one or two words that come to mind when you see the following car brands:

- Volvo
- BMW
- Tesla

You probably have vastly different opinions of each brand, and you're able to sum them up in an easy way. Something like the following probably came to mind:

- Volvo = safety
- BMW = performance
- Tesla = eco-conscious luxury

The perceptions and differentiation of each automotive brand are no accident. These are carefully cultivated positions, baked into the DNA of the way the cars are built, the branding, and the overall marketing strategy. The goal is for potential buyers to identify with the positioning of the car—from the first time they see a commercial to when they are drive it off the lot. They might not be able to articulate it, but they purchased that exact car because it's different from the others and it is valuable to the specific consumer.

Most of these car brands have been at work for years developing their differentiated position in a prospect's or customer's mind. Yet, it's been remarkable to see how Tesla has developed their brand differentiation in just a few short years. Everything about the Tesla experience, from the website to the test-drive, espouses something *different* about the car. They orchestrate a "high" to make you feel good about buying this vehicle. In most car buying situations, you walk onto the lot, are hounded by a salesperson, and go on a test-drive around the interstate and surrounding industrial streets where the car lot is located. Then you go back to their office, have a stressful negotiation session, and even if you do settle on a price, feel like you didn't get the best possible value. With the Tesla, everything is different from the moment you step into a high-end storefront to meet your associate for your appointment. Once in the car, they size you up and put on some music they think you would like, highlighting the gorgeous display dashboard. Then they take you for the most scenic drive in the area available. The whole experience feels like you're in a luxury car commercial. At the end, they show you the nonnegotiable price and the payment options. They've been able to differentiate not just by having an amazing product but by the way they bring the customer along the journey.

As product marketers, we often get the chance to help differentiate in the product build. What product marketer's own, however, is making sure the differentiation is highlighted through all marketing channels available—for example, through the Tesla test-drive experience.

A Taste of the Rockies

Sometimes you're in a market where the product is really commoditized (like many B2B SaaS, or software-as-a-service companies), and there's maybe only 2 percent differentiation in the product. What do you do then? One of my favorite examples of differentiation in a commoditized industry is Coors Light, an unexceptional light beer common in the United States and affectionately called C-minus by my husband. The main differentiator of Coors Light? It's ice-cold beer. You might be thinking, "Isn't being an ice-cold beer something all beers can be?" Why, yes! But Coors Light has leaned into this differentiated positioning so much that when you think about Coors Light, you think about having a refreshing ice-cold beer. What's amazing is the cold part is not even something they control—the customer must keep it cold!

Let's first examine their marketing and product development. One of their evergreen marketing campaigns is their association with the Rocky Mountains (brrrr) thanks to their location outside of Denver. The imagery surrounding any Coors Light ad is blue and silver—cold colors. In their advertisements, they often depict an explosion of a cheers between two beers with cold beer and condensed water dripping every which way. As for the product, they have doubled down on the ice-cold differentiation with their "cold-activated can" technology—when a Coors Light beer is cold enough to drink, the mountains on the can turn blue.

All of these efforts have given Coors Light the consistent number two position in the US domestic beer category, but they spend about 10 percent in marketing ($100 million annually) compared to the leader, Bud Light (owned by AB InBev, with a whopping annual budget of about $1.5 billion across all of their brands). Ready for a Coors Light yet?

Lyft versus Uber

One of my other favorite examples of differentiation is Lyft versus Uber. In the race to differentiate in the mid-2010s, they both had major ad campaigns to help you get a sense of their differentiation:

- Uber—Black and silver, sleek design. With the slogan, "The all-business way to get from A to Z." Uber's branding and messaging was all-professional.
- Lyft—Pink and a more approachable childlike design aesthetic. With the tagline, "Your friend with a car," Lyft's branding messaging was fun and friendly.

Both brands really doubled down on their differentiation for quite some time, with Uber offering more premium ride services, and Lyft encouraging their drivers to fist-bump when welcoming you into the experience. It was easy to tell what you were getting, and sometimes as a consumer, you might "feel" like taking a Lyft over an Uber because of this differentiation and vice versa. However, as both brands have scaled globally and gone public, they have commoditized and lost some of that initial differentiation.

Where You Can Differentiate

There are a few different ways you can differentiate your positioning in addition to product differences. These are:

- Branding—Colors, logo, font

- Industry—Choosing to focus on an industry that your competitors are not
- Buyer/Persona—Choosing a different buyer or user for your products than the competition
- Pricing—Premium versus value (note that you cannot differentiate on just the price—as mentioned, it needs to be a strategy)
- Customer Experience/Service Levels—This is an option, but be careful with this one not to over-promise and to have specific services customers get at each pricing level

Note that the marketing team can propose the original differentiation elements, but it's important to validate these with customers to make sure that they matter. For example, the main differentiation for a brand I was recently working with was that they were "transparent." Turns out, customers don't really care, and it wasn't affecting the buying decision at all.

How Do You Tactically Create Differentiated Positioning and Messaging?

Positioning and messaging shouldn't be done in a silo. The inputs are a combination of internal perspectives, customer research (as described in Part 2), the product details, any existing brand messaging, and an understanding of the competitive landscape. Read on for more perspectives.

LAUNCH LEARNING: The positioning and messaging you develop should be a combination of all of the research you've gathered about the market, competition, as well as internal perspectives.

When I'm initially developing on positioning for a product, I set aside a couple of hours when I can work without interruption. I look at all the research before me and review it all at once. Often, this is information I have already researched personally, but reviewing it all at once helps to uncover insights I may not have noticed before. I then fill in the positioning statement and messaging house line by line and come back to it after a few hours (or days) to see if I missed anything or want to rework any parts.

Then I grab a couple of the smartest people on the product, sales, and customer teams (keeping the group small, to max 3 other people per session) and have review sessions where I explain my rationale for the positioning and messaging and ask others to provide their input. Walking them through it rather than just sending them a document is much more valuable to the experience and always yields better results. From there, I usually go back and ask myself two questions: (1) Does the messaging and positioning roll up to "the why" of the company? (2) Is this messaging compelling or dull— do people care about the reasons we outlined to buy?

Once I've gotten sign-off on the high-level positioning and messaging, I work with a copywriter to develop the copy for each of my core external assets. I usually write the internal messaging, for sales and other teams, myself.

I review the messaging for style but also make sure I'm constantly comparing it to the positioning and messaging house and that it didn't get off track.

INTERNAL PERSPECTIVES

Leading the positioning exercise with members of your organization can be eye opening. I find internal perspectives to be invaluable to the product—if they are diverse. The first way you can get intel on creating your positioning statement is by sending out the "fill in the blank" statement in a Word doc, asking stakeholders from all different parts of the organization to fill it in and then comparing what you find to help develop the statement. I've done this successfully in meetings and workshops, by having each person read off what they wrote, writing everything on a whiteboard, and noticing the discrepancies. You might notice some major differences in points of view going through this exercise, but it's a great opportunity for discussion.

Another way I seek internal perspectives on positioning and messaging is to have everyone from the CEO to the "frontline" customer service representative fill out a questionnaire about the company or product (usually picking 5 people, no more than 10). From there, I can start to understand the core of the company and product, where they are, where they'd like to go, and specific language that they use to showcase the product. Once I receive their inputs, I gather the other research previously mentioned and fill in the positioning and messaging house for review. Here's an example of the worksheet I've used to quickly gather these types of internal perspectives (download your copy at Productlaunch.pro).

Messaging and Positioning Workshop

PARTICIPANT QUESTIONNAIRE

Submitted by: fill in name and role

- In 50 words or fewer: What problem does your product solve and why does it matter?
- Provide three words to describe your product or service today.
- What three words describe what you'd like your product or service's image to be one year from today?
- What other companies/brands would you like to emulate when it comes to cultivating a public image and/or eliciting an emotional response from current and prospective customers?
- What are your company's most novel and noteworthy attributes as a business?
- How would you plan to extend your product or service offering? What's the roadmap vision—near term, long term?

- Describe your typical customer(s) today. What do they DO? What do they HAVE (i.e., smartphone/car)? What do they THINK/FEEL? What frustrates them? What inspires them?
- How do you think typical customer(s) may change in the coming year(s)?
- Why should your ideal prospect buy from you over the competitors?
- What are the most compelling proof points you believe should be amplified in your messaging (e.g., where you source your ingredients, expertise, brand-name customers, business-related metrics, etc.)?

RAPID COMPETITIVE INSIGHTS

To understand how to differentiate your product either in the build phase or in the product marketing, you naturally must have a good grasp on the competition and the industry at large. However, don't mistake feature wars with differentiation. For differentiation to truly work, your product must holistically be seen as different from the competition, not just one feature here or there. I could write another book on competitive insights, but here's a quick way to get the information you are looking for.

After drafting up your positioning pillars (remember the house? Let's put that to use!), make a quick Excel matrix with the pillars and your top competitors. Then do the work to fill in how your competitors position themselves for each of those pillars. For example, your main benefits pillars might look something like this:

- Easy to use
- Fast onboarding
- Customer is in control (can make changes)

Take these three and map them out in a table to see how your competitors stack up. Do some light cyberstalking: look at competitive websites, note boilerplate statements (the statement at the bottom that usually contains location) from their most recent PR statements, review any new features they've come up with. If you see that you're saying exactly the same thing about your competitors, you need to go back to the drawing board.

	Comprehensive Service	Focused on Women	Great Selection
Competitor A	X		X
Competitor B			X
Competitor C		X	X

TAKEAWAYS

Creating positioning and messaging is a lot of work and requires alignment from everyone making decisions about the launch. Taking the time to get it right goes a long way in making sure your launch is successful.

- ✓ Product positioning should be done in parallel to the product build, not after the fact.
- ✓ Positioning should come before messaging. It is the perceived perception of your brand or product in a prospect's mind, usually on an internal document only.
- ✓ Messaging is the value you want to convey to a customer or prospect and can be found on all of the assets they would see.
- ✓ Defining differentiation is critical so customers and prospects know why to choose you over the competition.

✓ Positioning and messaging shouldn't be done in a silo. The inputs are a combination of internal perspectives, customer research (as described in Part 2), the product details, any existing brand messaging, and an understanding of the competitive landscape.

PART 5

DEFINE THE METRICS THAT MATTER

"You can't manage what you can't measure."

—**Peter F. Drucker**, management consultant, educator, and author

YOUR LAUNCH—DOES IT MATTER?

One of the launches I worked on at Google was a major, cross-functional campaign called RE:Brief, which we launched at SXSW. For the uninitiated, SXSW used to be THE sexiest place to launch any new product or company as everyone in the tech world seemingly descended to Austin, Texas for a week of illuminating tech talks, parties, breakfast tacos, and unlimited Shiner beers.

The concept of the campaign was to reimagine famous campaigns of the *Mad Men* era in a digital age and to promote new digital advertising tools that would have enhanced those legendary campaigns from yesteryear. We brought back the original creatives and copywriters, men and women now in their eighties and nineties, from several memorable campaigns, such as Volvo's "Drive It like You Hate It," Coca-Cola's "Buy the World a Coke," and Avis's "We're # 2 —We Try Harder."These are the Rembrandts and Picassos of the advertising world. The Google team shared reimagined digital concepts to these legends, which were based on the print and television ads they had created in the past, to get their feedback on how they would work in the modern age. We even made a documentary about the process. I played a small part, but as a new product marketer learning the ropes, it was a dream launch to work on.

My role was social media activation, which at the time was rather nascent. I built out a thorough plan, had it vetted by my stakeholders, and collected the right assets. On launch day, I coordinated our own content as well as retweets with media partners. We had millions of impressions, including an article and tweets from *The New York Times*. It felt like everyone was talking about the campaign at SXSW.

We celebrated all week (note: many Shiner beers were consumed).

Flash forward to the following week in our monthly marketing all-hands, where we had to present the results of the launch to management and the broader marketing team. I glowingly shared the results of our reach, impressions, and retweets. I'll never forget our director's response after I was done sharing my slides. She asked, "Does it matter?"

As you can imagine, I was pretty devastated, and after I flubbed my way through talking about reach and why social media matters, I had to admit to myself, I had no idea if it really mattered or not. And I vowed to never be in that situation again.

WHY IS MEASUREMENT SO DAUNTING?

Whether you are managing a launch or any other project, measurement is often a sore spot. For many of us, measurement is an afterthought or something slapped on at the end. But it should be part of your strategy and given as much thought as your overall GTM plan.

LAUNCH LEARNING: Measurement shouldn't be an afterthought but rather immersed throughout the launch process.

Measurement is challenging for product marketers for a few reasons:

- It's difficult to measure everything we do.
- We have many stakeholders with different goals.
- There are usually several variables and dependencies for any given project.

WHY IS MEASUREMENT SO IMPORTANT NOW?

Measurement is critical now for a simple reason: If it's not on Strava, it didn't happen.

Let me break this down a bit. Did you at any point today track your movement on Strava, a Fitbit, Apple Watch, or some other device? Yes? Me, too. I won't even get up to get a coffee unless I have my Fitbit on—I gotta get those steps in!

As consumers, we are in the age of measurement, tracking almost everything we do, from walking to meditation to every bite of food we eat. It's irresponsible to not bring that kind of thinking to your product marketing.

We can also do everything in almost real time. In the past, reports used to be gathered only every quarter and would vaguely inform the business strategy. Today, we can make changes based on metrics and iterate toward our strategy on the fly.

Additionally, product marketing has grown up as a role, and measurement is not only expected but required.

Product marketing has gone through a drastic change in the last few years. It's a relatively new role, maybe only 15 years old, and has just recently gained momentum. When product marketing first became a sought-after role, it seemed companies were unsure about how to leverage the position. Many knew they needed a product marketer but did not know how to maximize the role to its full potential. Now we're responsible for developing overall product messaging and frameworks, delivering personas executing product launches, ensuring there are impactful use cases, and working with customers to establish accurate data collection and solutions to their pain points. In addition, more and more, we're considered the general manager of a business and responsible for direct revenue as well. Today, stakeholders not only understand what we do but expect us to drive the business, and that requires measurement.

You Can't Manage What You Can't Measure

If your launches and other projects aren't rolling up to the metrics that matter, what are you celebrating? We spend so much time planning launches, creating GTM plans, and wrangling stakeholders, but if you don't have goals to level up to, how do you know that what you're working on is the right thing?

Non-revenue-generating teams are often on the chopping block. Product marketing is often revenue generating but struggles to prove it, and this is not okay.

The Product Marketing Alliance *State of Product Marketing 2020* report noted that product marketers feel they have a 6.3/10 influence on goals and strategy (this is unfortunately down from 6.5 in 2019). When thinking about the influence they have on the company overall, they rated a 6.8/10. That would be a D or an F in most grading rubrics. We can do better! One major way to up-level the influence of product marketing or the specific product launch you are owning is to have goals and metrics that are meaningful to the business overall.

LAUNCH LEARNING: Make product marketing more influential by aligning to goals and metrics that are meaningful to the business overall.

THE 3 STEPS TO METRICS SUCCESS

Now that you're on board and understand the why behind measurement, here's a tactical plan to get you to be more metrics driven in your approach, to launches, other projects you are working on, or even your entire PMM annual plan.

Let's explore each of the 3 Steps to Metrics Success:

1. Know Your Stakeholders
2. Choose Goals and Metrics Wisely
3. Build Your Measurement Plan

Know Your Stakeholders

Because product marketing sits in the middle of different organizations, you might have multiple people who you need to answer to and collaborate with. Ideally, with each launch, you would please everyone, but often you can't, so stack rank the stakeholders who are most important to you.

You know product marketers do so much more than just product launches. We work on market validation, positioning and messaging, GTM enablement, and content. How do we show what we're influencing and get our stakeholders to care as well? By speaking their language.

The following is what each of your top stakeholders care about overall and how you might frame your launch metrics to their thinking. Since we're product marketers, let's look at these in terms of personas.

If you are at a smaller company, you might be talking to the heads of each department. If you're at a larger company, you might not have access to the C-suite, but think of how these personas map to the person you are able to connect with.

Head of Product

Product managers are key stakeholders in the launch process. They are obsessed with how the product is used and if it's growing.

What they care about: How fast is product usage growing?

Top metrics:

- Product usage and adoption—How often are customers coming back (often expressed as MAU—monthly active use)?
- Product growth—How much has product usage increased over a given time period (e.g., month over month or quarter over quarter)?
- Churn/retention—Are customers sticking with us? Why/why not? Churn or retention can be expressed by attrition rate or retention rate, respectively.

For a new product, it would be easy to set product usage and adoption goals and to track growth and the effects on churn over time.

CMO

The CMO, head of marketing, or the marketing counterpart you work with (often content, demand generation, or both) is laser focused on customer growth and value. Sometimes you will work with a more brand-oriented marketing leader, but by speaking their language of leads, you will have their ear and support.

What they care about: How many new customers are we acquiring?

Top metrics:

- Leads—Are we on track to hit the marketing qualified leads (MQLs) we've committed to?
- Customer acquisition costs (CAC)—How much does it cost us to get a new customer?
- Customer lifetime value (CLTV)—What is the total value of our customers by segment?
- Annualized recurring revenue (ARR)—For subscription businesses, this is how much in revenue you can expect over the course of the year based on marketing's impact.

Head of Sales

Yes, you guessed it, the head of sales cares only about sales. Particularly, they care about their in-quarter topics and (if senior enough) how their pipeline is doing.

What they care about: Will we hit revenue goals?

Top metrics:

- Revenue—Will we hit quarterly or annual revenue targets?
- Time to close—How can I close deals faster?
- Pipeline—Are we set up for success?

Start the Conversation

Now that you know the right people to be talking to, the goal is to start the conversation about measurement early and ask the right questions. Most companies trip up because they don't ask the right questions before measuring. Doing this requires a collaborative partnership between analyst and product team, rather than a more traditional stakeholder-resource relationship.

Here are some example questions to get the conversation started:

- "I'm building my plan. What are your most important goals that we can align on?"
- "How can product marketing activities align to those goals?"
- "What matters most to you?"

Choose Your Goals and Metrics Wisely

To overcome the vagueness of measurement, choose the right top-level goals and understand the best metrics that can be tracked underneath those goals.

Hopefully, you have had conversations with your top stakeholders to understand the topline goals driving their business, but you can also learn from other product marketers. According to the 2020 Product Marketing Alliance, bottom-line KPIs are a top priority for product marketers: 58 percent are responsible for generating revenue, 45 percent are responsible for increasing marketing qualified leads, and 42 percent are responsible for retaining customers.

Bottom-Line KPIs Are a Top Priority for Product Marketers

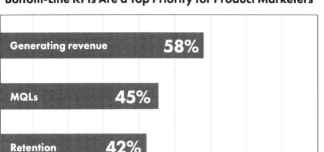

Here's an exercise to get you started.

First step: Choose 3 top-level goals and map them out as such:

Top-Level Goal	Grow Revenue	Increase Product Usage	Decrease Churn
Metric	**X**		**X**

Second step: Pick the leading indicators that PMM can influence and track underneath it such as:

- New feature adoption
- Content downloads

- Demo requests or views
- Product landing page conversion
- Product activation
- Adoption
- Sales pipeline increase
- Customer win rate increase
- Product usage tracking
- Internal and external surveys
- Sales cycle length
- Initial sale
- User adoption
- Trials
- Customer engagement metrics like content downloads and event attendance

Third step: Pick the leading indicators PMM can influence and track underneath the top-level goal. Here's an example of how that will play out:

Top-Level Goal	Grow Revenue	Increase Product Usage	Decrease Churn
Metric	Increased win rates	Monthly, weekly, or daily active users	Customer engagement metrics such as content downloads, customer event attendance

Here's a little more context on the metrics I chose.

Win rates—At Adobe, we regularly look at win rates, which helps us understand if our positioning and offer is working in market. Specifically, we look at these formulas:

- Accounts won/total pitches
- Won revenue/total potential revenue

Active users—Tracking product usage is likely a shared responsibility with product management, and product managers may also be tasked with improving certain usage metrics. At SocialChorus, I worked closely with our CTO to develop the product usage metrics we cared about, including monthly active users. And it was a goal the entire management team could rally around.

Content metrics—This is another metric that can map up to several higher-level goals, including retention, especially if you can deduce that content engagement like downloading a white paper or attending a customer event correlate with higher retention rates. You can usually track this by looking at cohorts of customers that do not take these actions and comparing them.

Build the Measurement Plan

Now that you know the top-level goals and the metrics PMM can influence, it's time to build out the measurement plan.

You might need to involve several teams (like marketing operations, your sales team, etc.) to get answers to the following, but to be successful, you need to know:

- What are the results of the metrics you have historically tracked?
- What are the mechanics of how you will track each metric you've committed to?
- How often will you communicate your progress to stakeholders?

Establishing a Baseline

Don't be afraid. Even if it's painful, you need to see where you are starting out. For each metric, map back to a specific time frame that will give you some data (e.g., a yearly, quarterly, or monthly view).

Next comes the delicate balance of goal setting with your stakeholders. I recommend taking a first pass based on what you know and sharing with the stakeholders to give them something to react to. You want the goals to be realistic but to not sandbag either. Think about a few things as you're setting your goals:

- What does your promotion plan look like?
- Will you have a large budget to promote?
- Will staffing (on your team, sales, or product/ engineering) be the same or different throughout the time frame?

What you end up with could look something like this:

	Increase Win % Quarterly	Product Usage— Monthly Active Users (AAUs)	Content Usage— Downloads
2021 Baseline	50%	5,000 MAUs	500 monthly white-paper downloads
2022 Goal	52%	6,000 MAUs	800 monthly white-paper downloads

Now you have a plan that you can share with your stakeholders and update as needed.

Channel Metrics and Plan

Channel metrics are specific objectives used to report on how each of your launch marketing channels is hitting committed goals. These content-level goals should map up to the higher-level goals that we set in the "key info" page of our GTM plans. Set these content-level goals based on historical performance or what you are really trying to achieve. I like looking at goals one week, one month, and three months out from launch, but you can just choose one time frame if that's easier.

Let's say your adoption goals tab are to get 500 customers using your product. Let's also imagine one of your main channels is email, and you have 10,000 people on your email list. A fantastic email open rate is 25 percent (2,500) and a great conversion rate (i.e., they take the action recommended, such as downloading a white paper) is 2 percent—that's only 200 conversions. You know from previous launches that prospects and customers need at least 3 touches with your company before the sales team will want to talk to them (known as a qualified lead). So time to work on your channel plan. Review Part 1 of this book for more ideas on external content promotion to build out the math of the channel plan that will help you achieve your ultimate goals.

TAKEAWAYS

If you didn't measure it, it might as well not have happened! This chapter shared how to overcome fear of measurement and create a plan that can align to your business goals.

- ✓ Measurement shouldn't be an afterthought but rather immersed throughout the launch process.
- ✓ Product marketing can be more influential by aligning to goals and metrics that are meaningful to the business overall.
- ✓ Product marketing often owns "leading indicator" goals like MQLs but also can be responsible for revenue and retention.
- ✓ Measurement is daunting, but it doesn't have to be. Break it down into knowing your stakeholders, choosing the right goals and metrics, and building your measurement plan.
- ✓ Don't be afraid—you have to start somewhere. Build out a baseline of the top leading indicator metrics that you know how to track, and use educated guesses to make predictions for the future if needed.

PART 6

NAIL THE LAUNCH TIMING

"Most of us spend too much time on what is urgent, and not enough time on what is important."

—**Stephen Covey**, author of *The 7 Habits of Highly Effective People*

Meeting the deadlines of the launch and staying on track with milestones are the most complicated parts of running a product launch. A survey I conducted to the Facebook group "Women in Product," which has a membership of over 27,000 product marketers and product managers in tech, revealed that members thought sticking to deadlines was the number one most difficult part about a product launch. Furthermore, hitting deadlines as marketers is critical, as you likely have real, nonrefundable money behind a launch date, such as with a media buy or an in-person event. In this chapter, I'll walk you through some expert ways to hit your deadlines on the first try.

I've found that being overprepared up front, organizing the right launch team, and overly communicating the launch date and any potential delays are the best way to stay on schedule.

> **LAUNCH LEARNING:** The best way to meet your launch deadline is to be hyper-organized, get the right team together, and frequently communicate the launch dates and any risks.

PMM INSIGHT: A LAUNCH TIMING STORY

A few years ago, I led a launch that went well and hit our deadline despite a number of technical and policy issues that were major risks to executing on time. The key to success was setting a strategy, being hyper-organized, and having the right team and communication channels. At AdRoll (now known as NextRoll), we were launching a new product called

Prospecting that also elevated us into a new category. Since this was such a big play for us, there was constant pressure from the executive level to get everything about the launch right, including hitting the launch date.

The Strategy

The initial strategy was to release globally in early June, right before the seasonal summer slowdown, so we could have the best chance of securing some press coverage (remember, press is never guaranteed) and tie the launch to a major annual customer event. We thought this would give us the best opportunity to "make a splash" and have the biggest reach possible to our customers and prospective customers.

The launch date was set months in advance to align with a large customer event we were having in New York, which would serve as our launch party. For anyone who has worked in events or tech, adding a physical event to a software launch makes things doubly stressful. With events (in-person especially), you are locked into an often nonchangeable date and nonrefundable deposit with the venue, as well as all the other inflexible things that come with hosting an event—printing physical materials, inviting guests, ordering the catering, and so on. A software-only release tends to be a little more fluid—it is a pain to change, sure, but you can do it all digitally. Think about the difference of changing the date of a wedding compared to changing the date of a Zoom get-together. It's a lot harder to change the date of an event than to change the date of a blog post. Combining a live event with the launch release made the pressure internally spike.

The Team

The first thing I did when discussing the launch date was to make sure we had an executive sponsor to keep the pressure on the product and engineering teams to deliver on time. In this case, our executive sponsor was the VP of engineering. He attended our weekly steering committee meetings to help identify any problems early and sometimes "translated" blockers from engineering to marketing and sales when things weren't going as planned. He reported to the CEO and could regularly communicate the development of the project to him and provide air cover if something tricky came up. Since his name was publicly on the line as well, he had incentive to make sure this launch went well. We also were lucky to have a program manager, someone from our business operations team, who kept our meetings running smoothly, with clear agendas and action items we followed up on each week. She also sent out a weekly recap to a wider distribution via email to keep everyone in the loop.

LAUNCH LEARNING: To have a successful product launch, start with the right team and ensure you have an executive sponsor.

The launch core team looked like this:

- **Exec sponsor** (could be any director or VP who is invested in your launch)—Responsible for removing high-level blockers and providing air cover to executives.
- **Head of product marketing** (me)—Responsible for launch strategy, communicating the strategy to leadership and other groups, removing blocker, and often "getting your hands dirty" with details.
- **Product marketer** (running the day-to day of the release)—Responsible for managing the GTM checklist, executing on all activities, and flagging to upper management when there are any blockers.

- **Head of product**—Responsible for getting the right engineering and product resources staffed and ultimately, the timely release of the product.
- **Product manager** (running the day-to-day of the release)—Responsible for managing the engineering team building the product and flagging to upper management when there are any blockers.
- **Business operations manager** (acting program manager)—Responsible for setting the weekly agendas, communicating weekly updates and action items, managing the master schedule (marketing and product), and following up on any agreed-on action items.
- **Legal representative**—Responsible for giving legal opinions, reviewing content (on the marketing side), and often reviewing data sharing on the product side or anything else privacy related. In our case, we had an in-house legal counsel on the core team.

Outside of the "steering committee," we had a launch team made up mostly of marketers and some heads of sales teams to get their perspective, keep them abreast of launch activities and any risks to the launch date, and to make sure everyone knew their role when the launch happened. This included:

- **Head of design**—Responsible for the "look and feel" of the new product launch including web, deck collateral, event design, and so on.
- **Web designer**—Responsible for new web pages and publishing the website at the agreed-on time the day of the launch.
- **Digital media team**—To ensure we released our new organic social, SEO, and digital marketing campaigns the day of launch.
- **Event marketing lead**—Responsible for our NYC event.
- **Content marketing lead**—Responsible for publishing blog materials and our longer-form white paper about the category of the new product.
- **PR liaison**—Responsible for working with our external PR agency, pitching the story, and finding the right PR strategy for us to go to market.
- **Regional counterparts**—Responsible for translating any materials and potentially launching the product uniquely in their market with their own events and content.
- **Legal**—If legal isn't in your steering committee, make sure they have representation here.

Responsible for giving their legal opinions, reviewing content (on the marketing side), and often reviewing data sharing on the product side or anything else privacy related.

- **Sales representatives**—Responsible for being the "voice of sales." Often, I wouldn't choose the highest-level leader here, but someone who would benefit a lot from the launch who has previously shown engagement with marketing so they'll be eager to give feedback and also communicate this to their teams.

Communication Channels

As I've mentioned throughout this book, communication is key, and 10 percent of your time should be spent communicating what you are doing to your stakeholders and the broader company. The more you communicate, the more you build confidence, and the less disasters will come up. Here's a peek at what worked for us to constantly communicate about the Prospecting launch:

- The GTM checklist, updated at least weekly and shared with every communication

- Weekly steering committee meetings for 6 months before launch
- Weekly email recaps
- 2 Slack channels—one for the steering committee, one for broader communications to keep other interested parties informed
- Executive decks for monthly executive check-ins on launch progress
- "Roadshow" deck to all teams (sales, marketing, regional teams, even engineering)
- Biweekly meetings with launch team for 3 months before launch
- Frequent presentations at all-hands meetings, even if just a 3-minute progress update

---

LAUNCH LEARNING: Meet any risks to the launch date head-on and coordinate with the right stakeholders to ensure the damage is as little as possible.

The Potential Problem

Things were on track until about 2 months before the release, when we realized there were some new privacy regulations in the EMEA (Europe, Middle East, and Africa) region that would need to be addressed before we released our product there. We realized this because our legal representative had been following recent legislation in Europe (another reason to make sure legal is included early and often). We were originally planning to launch in all markets at the same time; however, this latest information precluded us from doing so. After meeting with the EMEA team, we decided to give the product team 3 more months to work on some of the issues that prevented us from launching in their region. We opted to delay the launch in Europe only. This also gave us an opportunity to make a bigger splash in the European market by releasing in September compared to June. Much of Europe is vacationing in the summer, so launching in September with a big event helped us make more of an impact. As far as #launchfails go, this one was relatively low impact because we were able to catch it early and make a game plan. Had we not been so organized nor had the legal team member in our steering committee, it could have been catastrophic.

> **LAUNCH LEARNING:** Get your launch day checklist in order and share it broadly. This will mean *everything* the day of.

Day of Launch Checklist

Get your coffee ready—it's launch day! One trick I've learned over the years with so many stakeholders is that it's prudent to have a "day of launch" checklist with owners and specific times. The timing should start the night before, as sometimes you'll want your website to launch the product then. Here are some things you want to make sure are included with both the exact time and owner:

- Press release publishing on the wire
- Publishing the website (note: if not the night before, this should be early, around 5:00 a.m. EST)
- First advertisements go live
- Customer email
- Blog post publishing
- Internal Slack message/email (again, internal communications are extremely important!)

I'd also recommend waking up as early as the first item on your list to make sure it goes off without a hitch; after all, you're in charge.

LAUNCH LEARNING: Do not forget about internal communications—they are your internal customers. Rallying your employees to launch is as important as the release to external customers.

The End Results

After months of preparation, meeting weekly, communicating daily, handling every technical and policy issue that came our way, revamping the website, polishing the sales script, speaking at company all-hands meetings, talking to the press, making sure the regional teams were in the loop, I'm happy to say the launch was successful and on time! Launch day was a blur, but I do remember it included waking up at 5:00 a.m. EST to check on the website (which was 15 minutes late, so luckily, I could chat with the web designer to see what was going on), getting some great press, fielding about a million questions from the NYC sales team at a Q&A, opening some champagne in the office, and attending the customer launch party. There may have even been some late-night karaoke after the customer party; after all, we deserved to celebrate!

More than the celebratory launch day itself, the product proved wildly successful for our business. I credit the product team but also the amazing product marketing effort that went into making sure everyone was on the same page with their messaging and launch activities.

10 TIPS TO HIT YOUR LAUNCH DATE

1. Product Marketing Proposes the Launch Date

To manage a timeline, you first need to propose a launch date and back into it to make sure both you and the product teams have enough time to hit this goal. Product marketing should be the driver of the launch date, not product or engineering, but it should be collaborative. The launch date can be around a beta, or when the product is available to all customers, or even tied to a large marketing event—whatever you think is right for your initial launch moment. Consider things like seasonality (generally, August and December are really "checked-out" months for anything in tech, so I tend to avoid those), holidays, and workload that you and your team have already committed to. I've also noticed the days of the week matter—Tuesdays and Wednesdays tend to be the best days to launch to get maximum attention. If your company is global, be mindful of international considerations. Launching something in June might work in the United States, but in France, it is the start of the slower summer months when many people are on vacation and won't register your launch.

2. Back into It

After proposing an initial launch date, do some quick "back of the envelope" math with your calendar to make sure you will hit your milestones and the launch date. Here's an example of how the thought process might go: "If we are aiming for a June 15 launch, that means the alpha will need to wrap no later than February 15 and the beta by April 15 in order to hit that date." Gut check this with your product manager (PM); they may be able to give you better context and see if the timeline is reasonable. Put it in a timeline view to allow people to visualize it and see if they agree.

3. Get to Know Your Product Manager

The partnership with your PM will be critical to hit your launch date. PMs generally fall into 3 buckets when it comes to setting launch dates: aggressive, conservative, or clueless about how realistic their product launch timing is. The best way to understand how accurate your PM will be when predicting the launch date is to ask others who have worked with them in the past. I also ask the PM directly about their experience hitting launch deadlines. After years of working with PMs, I know that some are more aggressive: they overpromise on their launch dates and are never ready by the deadline. Others are more conservative, and you might find yourself pushing them to get the product to market. The phrase "Don't let perfect be the enemy of good" comes to mind when working with these types of PMs. The clueless group are inexperienced and need some hand-holding to help them understand how to get a product released. Once you've figured out which category your PM falls into, get aligned on what is reasonable for launch, and back into the date and any contingency plans.

One popular contingency plan could be launching as a beta, as opposed to a GA (general availability) release. Also, keep in mind the stage of the launch (e.g., alpha, beta, GA), as discussed in Part 1. I've worked with PMs who were nervous about the launch date because they were afraid it meant the product could never be improved on again. In tech, you are often able to add a "beta" to the product launch to grow awareness of it, but you give yourself an out if the product isn't perfect. Even Gmail was in beta for five years!

4. Get an Executive to Sponsor the Launch

Leadership support (ideally from a VP or executive) is critical not just for visibility but also for staying on track with the launch date. This is especially important if anything with real money behind it is dependent on the launch. Appointing an executive sponsor is a great way to add gravitas to the launch and makes sure the entire team is accountable for hitting their launch date. The added executive oversight can also make sure details of the launch get communicated properly to the right executives internally and that you will have help with any roadblocks that may arise.

5. Nail Internal Communication

Nailing the launch date really comes down to communication

and accountability. Effective communication means everyone on your team is in the loop regularly; this way, you can spot any issues before they become problematic. Whether your team responds best to weekly email updates, check-in meetings, or Slack meetings, keep it consistent. For larger launches, you might do all the above. Whatever way you choose to communicate, keep it consistent.

6. Write Effective Launch Timing Communications

To write effective launch timing communications, choose your channel wisely. If you have an email culture, don't force Slack, and vice versa. If some people use one platform and some use others, communicate via both. Every week (or at a cadence that makes sense for you), send out a communication on the same day and ideally at the same time—people will look forward to it. Don't be afraid to give it a little personality and make it fun to read. Some tips:

- Try to keep things templatized—subject lines, the update outline—it will help you send updates and also help your readers understand this is for the launch they care about. An example subject line: [Product Launch Update] 8 weeks until launch.

- Include an update on how many days until launch.
- Each communication should include launch progress across the board. Include marketing, product, roadblocks, and action items with owners called out.
- Keep your audience engaged by including interesting stats about the product development, product and marketing "sneak peek" screenshots, and/or customer quotes.
- Use the update as a feedback loop for product, messaging, even client feedback.

I often joke that 50 percent of a product marketers' job is writing effective "blurbs"—or 1-2-sentence communications to express everything that's happening with a launch. Get good at this and use Grammarly to make sure your launch communications are as effective as possible!

7. Have Better Meetings

Your launch meetings are a critical place to discuss the launch timing. I would start and end every meeting with the key dates for the launch. Thinking back to your RACI, you should consider having a "core" team meeting of the most important (responsible and accountable) people at least once a week, and of the larger, more general (consulted and informed) once a month. The latter will appreciate your respect for their time and make a point to attend the meetings. Always have a clear, consistent agenda (ideally sent out before the meeting) that covers updates, roadblocks, and action items so everyone knows what to do when they leave the meeting. Bonus if you can follow up with a recap communication.

8. Just Say No

When you're bringing more visibility to your launch, you might start getting requests for random things, such as one sheets or one-off blog posts from specific groups in your company. A rule to live by: "Say no before you say yes" (can I get this printed on a shirt, please?). Although this might sound counterintuitive, when you are working toward a deadline and goals you've already set, it's critical to make sure you don't get distracted with extra work. If the requests are outside of those goals, you need to say no to protect your deadline.

9. Be Accountable

Ultimately, YOU are responsible for the launch timing as the product marketer or project leader, and you should do everything in your power to hit the date or to communicate changes to the launch plan as soon as they arise. Accountability means you're able to follow up with the right people but also be able to understand if someone dropped the ball. Keeping others accountable will help you anticipate any blind spots or weak links in the project well before midnight on the night before the launch (hopefully!).

Additionally, make sure one person is the "owner," or the ultimately accountable party, for each deliverable. Without this, you might have trouble understanding who is really in charge or should be held accountable if the ball drops.

10. Align and Educate on the Metrics

Numbers speak and they make people listen. If everyone has agreed to the launch goals and the metrics you are defining as success, it's critical to bubble progress toward these goals up as frequently as possible to know if there are any causes for concern. For example, if not hitting the launch date means sales won't hit their quota for the quarter, suddenly, more engineering resources might appear to get you on track.

Pointing out metrics early and often will get everyone comfortable with speaking about the progress of the launch and what they need to do, while also taking the emotion and politics out of it.

TAKEAWAYS

Hitting the launch date is one of the most challenging and intimidating aspects about running a product launch. But with the right team, organization, and troubleshooting plan, you can drive the team to successfully hit the launch date you have in mind.

- ✓ The best way to hit your launch date is to be hyper-organized up front, getting the right team together, and frequently communicating the launch dates and any risks.
- ✓ Start with the right team and ensure that you have an executive sponsor for the launch.

✓ Meet any risks to the launch date head-on and coordinate with the right stakeholders to ensure the damage is as minimal as possible.

✓ Do not forget about internal communications— rallying your company/business unit to launch is as important as the release to customers.

✓ Get your launch day checklist in order; this will mean everything the day of.

✓ Ultimately, you are responsible for the launch timing.

CONCLUSION

"The way to get started is to quit talking and begin doing."
—**Walt Disney**

Throughout this book, I have laid out the steps necessary to lead a successful product launch that I wish would have been spelled out for me when I first started. You have been given templates, new tools to add to your toolkit, and a host of examples to set you up for success. Now it's up to you to build the plan, rally the team, and run a successful launch!

Hopefully, you now feel more confident with running a product launch. Whether you are planning your first launch or your hundredth, there are some universal truths to follow. First is make a plan and stick to it, using the GTM checklist or your own system as the "source of truth" for everyone to follow. Next is to choose your launch team wisely. Although you might be the most visible face of the launch, the team you'll be working with day in and day out is critical to the success of the overall launch. Make sure everyone understands their role (and importance) in the launch and has defined ownership to foster accountability. Third, communication is key, internally and externally. Remember that "10 percent of your time should be communicating about the launch," which might sound like overkill, but it's not. I have never once been told that people are sick of hearing about my launch plans; in fact, these exciting announcements that show progress just might give your entire business or company a new energy and something to rally around.

Also remember that your launch will not go perfectly. What's important is that you have a bird's-eye view to anticipate any potential issues, the right team to handle them, and the communication channels set to inform everyone of any potential risks. Last, remember to have fun! Launches are often the most memorable part of a product marketer's career, and you should take some time to enjoy the journey along the way.

Throughout your career, launches may continue to be an integral part of your job, or it may be one of many areas you excel at. Either way, becoming proficient in launches requires a valuable skillset that you can translate to many other types of jobs. The core of hyper-organization, internal influence, and high communication will always be valuable.

Now that you've finished reading, I encourage you to apply the tools that work for you to your next launch. In the spirit of feedback, I'd love to hear from you—what worked, what didn't, and what you'd like to see more of. You can reach me on LinkedIn or at my email address MaryShirleySheehan @gmail.com.

Best of luck to you!

RESOURCES AND APPENDIX

RESOURCE: LAUNCH LEARNINGS

Check out all the Launch Learnings sprinkled throughout the book.

Launch Learning: The go-to-market (GTM) plan is more than a checklist—it's the strategy for how a company will target its customers and prospective customers with its value prop and differentiation from the competition with a product.

Launch Learning: Without a GTM plan, new products in market will leave marketing and sales scrambling and customers confused.

Launch Learning: I prefer to use Google Sheets to easily keep shareholders in the loop with what's happening and to receive and respond to comments on the plan.

Launch Learning: "Product/market fit means being in a good market with a product that can satisfy that market."—Marc Andreesen

Launch Learning: Ask the "dumb question" if you're not sure—"who is this product for?"

Launch Learning: No matter what approach you take to get to know your customers, put a plan together, get buy-in from stakeholders, and communicate the results.

Launch Learning: There is a lot of value from personally running the interviews, or at least listening to recordings. You can note specific words they use for future messaging, moments of hesitation, or moments of excitement. Be close to this part of the research.

Launch Learning: As the launch leader, you can be the agent of change to select as diverse a group as possible for your launch team.

Launch Learning: Ten percent of your time should be spent communicating about your launch internally.

Launch Learning: Use the best internal communication channels for your launch updates, and make the message sticky and exciting!

Launch Learning: The most successful product marketers become partners with product management teams, not "order takers."

Launch Learning: Product positioning should be done in parallel to the product development, not after the fact.

Launch Learning: Seek approval from executives (or the most senior people involved in your launch) on the positioning and messaging only. Let them know that once this is agreed on, the copy will be developed directly from these assets, but you don't want to burden them with reviewing every deliverable.

Launch Learning: Measurement shouldn't be an afterthought but rather immersed throughout the launch process.

Launch Learning: Make product marketing more influential by aligning to goals and metrics that are meaningful to the business overall.

Launch Learning: The best way to meet your launch deadline is to be hyper-organized, get the right team together, and frequently communicate the launch dates and any risks.

Launch Learning: To have a successful product launch, start with the right team and ensure you have an executive sponsor.

Launch Learning: Meet any risks to the launch date head-on and coordinate with the right stakeholders to ensure the damage is as minimal as possible.

Launch Learning: Get your launch day checklist in order and share it broadly. This will mean *everything* the day of.

Launch Learning: Do not forget about internal communications—they are your internal customers. Rallying your employees to launch is as important as the release to external customers.

PMM RESOURCES

Here are some of my other favorite resources for learning more about product launches and product marketing.

COMMUNITY/CONNECTIONS

Women in Product Marketing podcast—The podcast I host, featuring top women in product marketing and beyond. Each week focuses on a different core topic of product marketing, career journeys, and what it's like to be a woman in tech.

Sharebird—A peer-to-peer networking resource for PMMs that features AMAs (Ask Me Anythings), and a variety of PMM podcasts, including the one I host—*Women in Product Marketing*.

Product Marketing Community—They have digital events and great content.

Product Marketing Alliance—A one-stop shop for PMM certification, content, and checking out the who's who of product marketing.

Pragmatic Marketing—This is the gold standard of PMM training and certification. Often, companies will pay for it as part of a training budget, so make sure you ask!

RESEARCH

Competitive intel—Check out G2Crowd, Owler, and set up Google Alerts for getting a quick review on competitive intel.

Google Forms are great for quick and scrappy survey research, especially internally. Typeform is another option that is super intuitive and looks great on mobile.

Calendly works well for scheduling customer interviews.

Vancery is a great recruiting platform to interview industry experts.

BLOGS/BOOKS

Intercom blog—They do great product marketing. Check out some of their resources on Jobs to Be Done (JTBD), which really changed my thinking. I've done several JTBD projects now.

Product Marketing Debunked—My friend and former colleague Yasmeen Turayhi wrote a great primer on being a PMM with an emphasis on market validation.

April Dunford's positioning book *Obviously Awesome.*

David Aaker is old school but a great resource on branding and positioning.

Play Bigger: How Pirates, Dreamers, and Innovators Create and Dominate Markets by Dave Peterson, Al Ramadan, Christopher Lochhead, and Kevin Maney—About creating a category king (also a really fun read).

Making Movies by Sidney Lumet—A bit out of the box, but there are a surprising number of parallels between making movies and being a successful PMM.

APPENDIX: ADDITIONAL DETAILS

External promotion—a more detailed view

Channel	Reasons for using	Cost	Tier
Organic digital—search engine optimization (SEO)	Long term—strategic initiative to help web customers find you organically online	$$$	1
Press—hire a PR agency or someone internal to pitch	Use press for a major product launch or a company launch. Many startups think they can just "email some reporters" to get press, but it's challenging to get a reporter to write about you without the help of skilled professionals.	$$$$	1
Written case studies and testimonials	If you have clients who have already tried your product (i.e., beta testers) and who will speak for you, get them to! Ask for a simple quote (or write one and have them approve it) with their logo for something low key, or interview them and create a written case study with the content.	$–$$	1
Paid digital—search engine marketing (SEM), display ads, or video ads	Videos of customers singing your praises are extremely effective but can be very time intensive and expensive. You'll need help with the questions and maybe a script, and a professional videographer and editor.	$$$$	1

Video case study	If you're new to a market and your website is brand new, I highly recommend using paid ads. Doing it yourself can be time intensive but on the less expensive side, or you can hire someone.	\$ – \$\$\$	1
In-product messaging for product releases	Give existing customers a heads-up about a new product or feature. Tools like Pendo, Amplitude, and AppCues are great for product messaging on the fly.	\$ – \$\$	1, 2
Blogs and social posts	Blogs and social posts are great to drive awareness of your product and/or company online. They should be an ongoing staple of your marketing strategy because they help you build up SEO and create a reason to contact your customers. Hire a writer in-house or outsource this.	\$	Tier 1, 2
Content update for website	If you have an existing website, you should absolutely update the product content as part of your launch strategy. If you don't have a website, you can easily build out a basic one with tools like WordPress and Wix.	\$ – \$\$\$	1, 2

External email announcement	Emails should always be a staple of your product or company launch. Collect emails everywhere you can (legally!)— on your website, at events, and so on, and always continue to build this list.	$	1, 2
Update help center content	If you have a help center or knowledge base, it is a best practice to consistently update content once new features and products become available. This not only helps to promote your product but also makes sure customers can learn more about the "how to" and to trouble-shoot if needed.	Free	1, 2, 3

Sales enablement channels—more details

Sales enablement	Reasons for using	Time to produce	Tier
All-hands announcement	Many companies have weekly all-hands meetings; this is a great way to make sure sales and other business units know the key dates and the high-level picture about your launch.	Low	1
Goals/ incentives	Work with sales leadership to develop specific KPIs and incentives around selling this specific product or feature.	Med	1
One sheet	Creating a high-quality one sheet to send to prospects and customers can be an effective follow-up for sales, but it can also take a surprisingly long time to get right. You need to think about design, high-quality screenshots, and the right messaging and positioning. Save this for your highest-priority launches, or you will have to build them all the time.	Med– High	1
Sales certification	If the product is complicated or changes the positioning of your company, consider doing a sales certification. Usually, this requires creating a pitch script and a rubric. Salespeople pitch and/or demo the product to leadership, and only when they "pass" can they sell it.	High	1

Talking points/ pitch script	Talking points or a full pitch script can be valuable for more complicated products.	Med	1
Posting of materials to asset management system (intranet, Google Drive folder, etc.)	Make sure that whatever you create lives in the system that sales accesses regularly. If they don't have one, start a Google Drive or Dropbox folder with launch assets.	Low	1, 2
Sales training	Sales training is a must-have to make sure the sellers understand both the what and the why of the new product or feature. Without this, salespeople will say whatever they want about the product.	Med– High	1, 2
Slides	Creating a few slides about the product is a quick way to get sales the info they need about a product and help them incorporate it into their existing pitch deck.	Low– Med	1, 2
Comm doc/ internal FAQ	This internal document is a must-have for any launch as it is your "single source of truth." If possible, work with the product manager (PM) on this document and always keep it updated with new product information and assets.	Low– Med	1, 2, 3

Product stage definition

Stage	Goals	When to move on to next stage	Launch activities
Market validation—"homework" stage	Establish a hypothesis of product/market fit (including target market) Understand if the product is something we should pursue Dive deep into the competitive landscape	Assess that there is a good chance of product/market fit Understand the competitive landscape and how your product can stack up	Assess that there is a good chance of product/market fit with market research: deeply interview prospective customers and review the competitive landscape
Alpha—evaluation stage	Work closely with a handful of customers (fewer than ten) Validate the initial concept Iterate to a minimum viable product (MVP) May decide not to pursue at this stage	X number of live, happy customers Commercialization planning with PMM International markets evaluated	Start building out a GTM plan Develop initial messaging, including positioning statement and unique selling propositions Set launch goals and expectations Develop target market personas "Bare bones" launch content produced: sales comm doc, product one sheet, deck

Closed beta— testing with customers	Start driving adoption through demand generation or selling efforts Start selling into international markets Iterate product to fit market needs Test marketing messaging and provide sales collateral Create KPIs/ gates for moving to the next stage	Specific KPIs achieved Large number of clients are live and loving it (all verticals/ segments tested) Comprehensive testing delivered Pricing model finalized GTM plan finalized	GTM plan finalized Pricing developed and tested Finesse target market personas Messaging tested with prospects and through channels like website Launch content continues—build out product web page, demo videos Build out educational content such as webinars Start speaking to customers for testimonials
Open beta— testing with customers through sales	Sales is able to sell at their discretion All marketing materials are available and localized Self-serve UI being tested on a percentage of customers Potential marketing push	KPIs maintained and achieved Self-serve UI ready to go live globally Product works at scale GTM plan initiated	

GA—full global launch	Product is available for all customers		Product "launch" date happens, PMM manages "day of launch" calendar and coordinates with other marketing teams (PR, events) as well as product and sales

ACKNOWLEDGMENTS

Although I would love to say that this was my "quarantine project," this book has been a labor of love, almost four years in the making. I originally started writing when I was consulting full time and had a much more flexible schedule. Three jobs and two kids later, I'm proud that this has finally come to fruition. There were many friends, family members, and product marketers who encouraged and supported me along the way and who really kept me going. Thank you for caring about this project.

I want to especially thank my first reader and editor, Prachi Mishra, for taking the time to read this book (over and over) and giving me some compelling ways to make it better.

I'd also like to thank my husband, Patrick, for believing in me, pushing me to finish this, assisting with the design, and of course, sacrificing his own "free" time to hang out with our son so I could finish this. I love you to the Truckee River and back.

Thank you to my dad, Rob Shirley, who has always been an inspiration to me in business, and to my grandmother Ruth Shirley, who published her first book at age 85.

I'd also like to thank my favorite designers, Richard Koscher, who came up with the original cover designs for this book, and my cousin Shannon Thorpe, an up-and-coming designer who produced many of the original images for this book.

I also want to thank the community of listeners and guests of my podcast *Women in Product Marketing*, who have been encouraging and inspirational along this journey.

Made in the USA
Monee, IL
12 February 2023